MEMORANDUM O
TEACHING OF EN

MEMORANDUM
ON THE
TEACHING OF ENGLISH

Issued by the Incorporated Association of
Assistant Masters in Secondary Schools

NEW AND REVISED EDITION

CAMBRIDGE
AT THE UNIVERSITY PRESS

1927

CAMBRIDGE
UNIVERSITY PRESS

University Printing House, Cambridge CB2 8BS, United Kingdom

Cambridge University Press is part of the University of Cambridge.

It furthers the University's mission by disseminating knowledge in the pursuit of education, learning and research at the highest international levels of excellence.

www.cambridge.org
Information on this title: www.cambridge.org/9781107594395

© Cambridge University Press 1927

First published 1927
Re-issued 2015

A catalogue record for this publication is available from the British Library

ISBN 978-1-107-59439-5 Paperback

PREFACE

TO THE

REVISED EDITION

THE publication of this Memorandum in 1923 was immediately followed by a demand for copies, which showed that the need for the kind of guidance which it provided was great. Indeed, the first impression was quickly exhausted and two further ones were necessary. These, too, have also been exhausted. The Executive Committee of the Association responsible for the publication decided that, before another edition was printed, the Memorandum ought to be brought up to date, and they placed the revision in the hands of the Sifting Sub-Committee of the original Committee. Unfortunately, the Sub-Committee was unable to obtain the assistance of Mr J. F. Usherwood, who was to such a great extent responsible for the success of the original Memorandum. Another member of the Sub-Committee, Mr T. Crockett, is now a Headmaster and his help also was not available. Nor could Mr Lissant, now a House Master, attend meetings. Consequently, nearly all the work of the revision has fallen upon the shoulders of Messrs Palser and Phillips, who received, however, valuable assistance from Mr Goodman.

The Sub-Committee, following the lines upon which the Committee worked in 1922, issued Questionnaires to all members of the full Committee and the revision is based upon the replies received.

But few alterations have been made in the first two chapters. It was found necessary to rearrange Chapter III, and a very full treatment of Précis—hardly touched in 1923—has been added. Chapter IV, however, has been entirely replanned and new matter added, including an interesting experiment on the teaching of composition through story-writing and a third list of books read. A separate chapter has been assigned to School Examinations. It contains a considerable amount of additional matter, including lists of modern essays, novels, and drama which correspondents consider typical of what should be read for First School Examinations.

Not the least valuable part of the original Memorandum was its Bibliography. This has been enlarged to nearly double its former size by the addition of books published since 1923 and of others also found useful by correspondents. The Sub-Committee desires to acknowledge fully its indebtedness to the publishing firms, over twenty in number, who so kindly placed at its disposal copies of all books in the least likely to be of service to readers of the Memorandum. The Bibliography has been rearranged on a somewhat elaborate plan which the Sub-Committee hopes will enable users to find readily their exact requirements.

Two valuable aids in the teaching of English are School Drama and Home Reading. Two Appendices have been added: the one consists of an account of the origin and development of a School Dramatic Society; the other of a very elaborate scheme, now in actual working, for Home Reading. Both have been specially written for this revision of the Memorandum.

J. H. ARNOLD

CHAIRMAN

The Revising Committee desires to express its appreciation of the assistance which it received from Miss K. M. Edwin, who acted as secretary.

PREFACE

TO THE

ORIGINAL EDITION

ORIGIN AND AIM OF THE MEMORANDUM

IT has long been evident to all thoughtful people interested in education, and not least to teachers, that English instead of being the very foundation of all education in this country has, in practice, received but scant attention when questions of organisation and curriculum have been decided. The fact is hardly in dispute, and is supported by paragraph after paragraph of the epoch-making Report of the Departmental Committee of the Board of Education published at the end of 1921 (*The Teaching of English in England*). One quotation may serve as typical: "From the evidence laid before us it became speedily clear that in many schools of all kinds and grades that part of the teaching which dealt directly with English was often regarded as being inferior in importance, hardly worthy of any substantial place in the curriculum and a suitable matter to be entrusted to any member of the staff who had some free time at his disposal" (pp. 9, 10).

This inferior position held by English has certainly not been due to lack of capability, or lack of interest on the part of the teachers specially responsible for the organising of the English teaching in the schools. Investigations have shown what originality, what zeal, what readiness to try new ideas and to sacrifice time and energy in promoting the success of their work these teachers possess. The fault has lain almost wholly in lack of sympathy on the part of the school authorities, shown partly by a failure to allot adequate time to the subject and partly by a reluctance to give the Senior English Master the same power of supervision and of direction as is given to the Senior Classical, Modern Language, Mathematical, or Science Master. The increased cost of books, too, especially in these days of strict economy, presses more heavily on those who are striving to make English an instrument of true education than on any others.

Teachers have long known how unsatisfactory the position has been; the importance of the Departmental Report lies largely in the fact that it has focussed attention upon the handicap from which English teaching has suffered. Not only has the educational world been forced to stop and give the matter consideration, but the more thoughtful section of the lay press has tried to interest public opinion. The Departmental Committee indeed, to paraphrase the words of Siéyès, found English nothing and will only be content when it is everything. Such enthusiasm is bound to produce results, for a more eloquent yet reasoned appeal for English to be put into its rightful place could hardly have been written.

Dealing with the teaching of English in all stages of education from the Elementary School to the University, the Departmental Committee indicated very clearly the aims which teachers should place before themselves and the general lines along which they should proceed. It made little attempt, and it could hardly have done otherwise, to translate theory into practice, to help the actual teacher to apply, in the classroom and elsewhere, the principles so admirably laid down in its Report. *What* should be done was rendered abundantly clear; *how* it could best be done was a problem which had obviously to be faced by the teachers themselves.

Accordingly, in January, 1922, the Incorporated Association of Assistant Masters in Secondary Schools set up a Committee whose terms of reference were "to endeavour to reduce to system the various and often ill-defined methods of teaching English which at present obtain in English and Welsh Secondary Schools." This Committee consisted of some eighty members of the Association, practically all specialists in the teaching of English and representative of every type of Secondary School: Preparatory, Public, Endowed, Grammar, County, and Municipal. It has worked in two sections: a Corresponding Committee whose members supplied records of their various methods and experience, and a Central Committee which, after correlation by a smaller Sifting Sub-Committee, used these results as a general basis for discussion and conclusion.

This Memorandum must be regarded not as an essay on ideal aims but as a plain summary of experience, complementary to the Departmental Report; it embodies the considered opinions of the members of the Committee on methods of teaching English in Secondary Boys' Schools. It is not claimed that the methods here advocated are exhaustive; the members of the Committee would be the first to agree that they are not, for they are fully aware indeed that investigation and experiment are daily bearing good fruit. They recognise, too, that more perhaps in the teaching of English than in that of any other subject in a school curriculum, the most successful teachers are born, not made; yet they venture to hope that the Memorandum will be of some service to other teachers in Secondary Schools, particularly to younger men who may find a value in this brief summary of the experience of practical teachers who have had to face the actual difficulties inherent in classroom teaching.

It should be noticed that often, to the considered opinion of the Committee as a whole on some point, there are appended quotations from the opinions of individual members. These represent the record of personal experience, and as such are of extreme value, but the Committee, though approving of them in general, does not necessarily endorse every detail.

Of the two appendices to this Memorandum, one deals with the Report of the Joint Committee on Grammatical Terminology and the other consists of a Bibliography.

The Committee desires, here, to thank the numerous Educational Publishers for their generosity in placing at its disposal an almost overwhelming selection of books for its consideration. Of the books mentioned in the Bibliography all have been either carefully examined by the Sifting Sub-Committee, or specially recommended by members of the Committee itself as of proved value either to teacher or to class.

The success or failure of the work of any such Committee as this must always depend, to a considerable extent, upon its Honorary Secretary. In this case the Committee was fortunate in that it had the assistance of a specialist of ability and sound judgment. It wishes to express its deep appreciation of the work of Mr J. F. Usherwood, to whose energy is due to a large extent whatever value the Memorandum may possess.

CONTENTS

Page

PREFACE TO THE REVISED EDITION . . . v

PREFACE TO THE ORIGINAL EDITION . . . vii

MEMBERS OF THE ORIGINAL COMMITTEE . . xiii

Chapter

I. SOME GENERAL CONSIDERATIONS . . . 1
- TIME ALLOTTED TO ENGLISH 1
- THE CHARACTER OF HOMEWORK 2
- CORRELATION WITH OTHER SUBJECTS . . . 3
- GOOD ELOCUTION 3
- PHONETICS 4

II. THE TEACHING OF GRAMMAR 5
- THE CASE FOR GRAMMAR TEACHING . . . 5
- UNDER THE AGE OF 11 6
- THE AGE 11-13 9
- FROM THE AGE 13 ONWARDS 10

III. THE WRITING OF ENGLISH 11
- SPELLING 11
- METHODS OF INCREASING VOCABULARY . . . 11
- THE CORRECTION OF ERRORS IN COMPOSITION . . 12
- UNDER THE AGE OF 11 12
- THE AGE 11-13 14
- THE AGE 13-16 16

IV. THE READING AND APPRECIATION OF ENGLISH 26
- GENERAL REMARKS 26
- UNDER THE AGE OF 11 30
- THE AGE 11-13 33
- THE AGE 13-16 35
- EXPERIMENT AND EXPERIENCE 42

V. ENGLISH IN EXAMINATIONS 53
- THE FIRST SCHOOL EXAMINATION 53
- SECOND SCHOOL EXAMINATION: HIGHER CERTIFICATE . 59

APPENDIX I. A SCHOOL DRAMATIC SOCIETY . . . 64

APPENDIX II. A HOME READING SCHEME . . . 69

APPENDIX III. THE REPORT OF THE JOINT COMMITTEE ON GRAMMATICAL TERMINOLOGY 75

APPENDIX IV. BIBLIOGRAPHY 77

MEMBERS OF
THE ORIGINAL COMMITTEE

H. S. ADAMS	London Orphan School, Watford.
E. E. ALLEN	Tollington School, Muswell Hill.
D. ANDREW	Wrexham County School.
†*J. H. ARNOLD (*Chairman*)	St Dunstan's College, Catford.
HARTLEY BATESON	Municipal School, Oldham.
A. BRERETON	Friends' School, Saffron Walden.
*H. L. CONSTABLE	Central Foundation School, E.C.
J. W. COVE	Whitgift Middle School, Croydon.
W. COX	Hanson Secondary School, Bradford.
†*T. CROCKETT	Holloway County School, N. 7.
Rev. W. A. DAVENPORT	Grammar School, Carlisle.
M. W. DAVIES	Grammar School, Macclesfield.
J. C. DENT	St Albans School, Herts.
W. H. EDWARDS	Palmers School, Grays.
*A. R. ENTWISTLE	County School, Braintree.
*E. FOXON	The Grammar School, Loughborough.
G. H. GATER	City Boys' School, Leicester.
B. R. GIBBS	The Grammar School, Ashburton.
*W. GOODLET	Municipal School, Lincoln.
†*G. N. GOODMAN	County School, Ealing, W. 5.
*B. GROOM	Clifton College, Bristol.
W. HADLEY	Holborn Estate Grammar School, W.C.
H. W. HAMPTON	County School, Llanelly.
E. H. HARRIS	Rivington and Blackrod Grammar School, Lancs.
W. J. HUGHES	Normal College, Bangor.
E. E. KIRBY	The Grammar School, Kettering.
L. H. LEADLEY	Archbishop Holgate's Grammar School, York.
M. R. LE FLEMING	Durham School.
M. M. LEWIS	William Ellis School, N.W.
D. L. LIPSON	Cheltenham College.
†*S. P. LISSANT	Epsom College.
S. E. MALTBY	Sidcot School, Winscombe, Somerset.
J. W. MOLES	Rutherford College, Newcastle-on-Tyne.
*G. NEWTON	Alderman Newton's School, Leicester.
W. J. OSBORNE	County School, Abertillery.

* Members of the Central Committee.
† Members of the Sifting Sub-Committee.

G. W. PAGETT	Gillingham Technical Institute.
†*E. M. PALSER	Westminster City School, S.W.
M. T. PERKS	The Grammar School, Wakefield.
†*B. J. PHILLIPS	Caterham School, Surrey.
*C. H. PORTER	Tiffin Boys' School, Kingston-on-Thames.
F. H. PRITCHARD	Devonport High School.
J. W. PROUD	Coopers' Company School, Bow, E.
*F. J. RAHTZ	Cotham Secondary School, Bristol.
A. J. J. RATCLIFF	The Grammar School, Wallasey.
*R. A. RAVEN	Rugby School.
*R. E. RIGG	Mathematical School, Rochester.
F. E. ROBERTS	Central Secondary School, Sheffield.
C. J. ROBSON	Deacons' School, Peterborough.
W. J. SAULL	Coopers' Company School, Bow, E.
J. G. SIMPSON	The Grammar School, Ilkley.
H. G. SMITH	King Edward's School, Camp Hill, Birmingham.
L. C. SMITH	St Paul's School, W.
*A. C. SOUTHERN	Colfe Grammar School, Lewisham, S.E.
A. SPENCER	King Edward VI School, Retford.
*T. STAVELEY	Tonbridge School.
*W. J. STOKES	George Dixon School, Birmingham.
C. THACKRAY	Heckmondwike Secondary School.
H. THOMAS	The Grammar School, Carmarthen.
W. J. THOMAS	Simon Langton School, Canterbury.
†*J. F. USHERWOOD (*Hon. Secretary*)	St Dunstan's College, Catford.
H. VICARS WEBB	Bristol Cathedral School.
H. VINCENT YOULE	Secondary School, Heanor.
*A. M. WALMSLEY	Northampton School.
W. B. WHITBREAD	Tiffin Boys' School, Kingston-on-Thames.
*E. W. WILTON	Strand School, Brixton, S.W.
E. C. WILTSHIRE	The Grammar School, Hampton.
W. A. WOOLF	County Secondary School, Ramsgate.

* Members of the Central Committee.
† Members of the Sifting Sub-Committee.

CHAPTER I

SOME GENERAL CONSIDERATIONS

BEFORE dealing with any particular aspects of English teaching in practice, the Committee felt it necessary to clear the ground with regard to certain points which are not separately perhaps of extreme importance, but about which there must be some agreement if what follows is to be clear and of real value.

Time allotted to English

It is evident that time must, to some extent, be the crux of the whole position, and that it is hopeless to expect progress, or good work, where a quite inadequate amount of time is allotted to the teaching of English.

At present there is the greatest variety in time, ranging from $7\frac{1}{2}$ hours allowed in one Secondary School to some young boys who were not learning a second language, to $1\frac{1}{2}$ hours in the case of some boys of 15 in a London Secondary School. In the opinion of the Committee the following times are the minima, if its recommendations are to be carried out:

Boys under 11	5 hours a week.
Boys 11–13 ...	4 hours a week, and more if English is the only language studied.
Boys 13–16 ...	$3\frac{3}{4}$ hours a week.

N.B. These are actual hours, not periods, and should not include time given to Scripture, History, or Geography.

Teachers complain less of the scanty time at their disposal than of the practice of dividing the English work in particular forms among several men. However difficult it may be to arrange in the time-table, it is essential that all the English work in any one form, or set, should be taken by the same teacher; literature, grammar, reading, writing, discussions, are all phases of the same subject, and should never be taught in water-tight compartments. At the same time it must be recognised that one specialist, or even several, cannot take all the

English work in a large school; some of it will be in the hands of non-specialist masters.

A wise distribution of periods is quite as important as their number. To take one example, linked periods are useful, probably essential, in Science: they should never be permitted in the permanent time-table for English, but may occasionally be arranged for the completion of a lengthy dramatic reading or debate.

The Character of Homework

Broadly, there is a marked cleavage between those who would have homework mainly a repetition of work done in class, and those who value it as an opportunity for quiet original work done in a different atmosphere from that of the classroom. Probably neither opinion is always right; classes vary, individual boys vary, and, above all, homes vary. As a rule, homework in the lower part of the school should be of the first type—intended to drive home and reinforce something taught in class, but opportunities should always be given for the boy who can do good original work to do it away from school. It is a useful plan to set this some time (say a fortnight) before it has to be shown up, so that there is an opportunity for reference to books, or other authority, and for thought. It is quite common to set an original composition every week for homework; experience shows that this is too often. Letters, dialogues, short scenes between characters are suitable exercises for homework. Purely descriptive work, too, is nearly always better done at home.

It may be practicable in the lowest forms to set aside the last one or two periods of the day for preparation under proper supervision. In several schools this plan has been tried with success.

In the upper part of the school, naturally, the character of the homework will change. More original work will be expected, whether it consists of reading something not previously considered in class, or of writing, unaided, essays or compositions. Even here, however, it is the proportion which should be changed, and not the principle; there should still be a certain amount of work which will test attention, care, understanding, apart from originality.

Correlation with other subjects

In educational circles, a short time ago, "correlation" was a blessed word which had only to be pronounced to attract attention and command respect. There has been a reaction, and English masters have found that in the name of correlation they are expected to do work which is not their concern only. What is wanted is not so much formal correlation as a greater sense of co-operation, which will make much incidental correlation practicable and desirable. English will help History by encouraging the reading of historical novels, just as History will give the background for much of the reading; at the same time the English teacher must not be cramped by being confined to the literature of a short period of History. Grammar teaching offers another opportunity for co-operation, which does not mean that the English master alone should be held responsible for sound conceptions of grammar. It is the great recommendation for the adoption of a Common Terminology that it makes easier such co-operation; for often the English master can illustrate or emphasise points by reference to other languages. To take a very simple example, the French *canne à pêche* clinches the argument, for a boy who knows some French, that "fishing" in the compound word fishing-rod is a gerund and not a participle.

The Science or technical teacher will often be able to suggest subjects for essays, not necessarily purely descriptive, but embracing wider views. For example, to ask boys on the technical side of a school to write on "The qualities necessary to a successful engineer" will be helpful to the English master, for there will be some chance for originality and enthusiasm, while it will help the Engineering master by lifting his subject from the plane of mechanical detail, and concentrating, if only for a space, on ulterior aims.

Good Elocution

Nothing is more important in these days of careless pronunciation than to encourage the correct speaking of English. Throughout the school course this aim must be kept in view, to be realised not only through reading aloud and repetition, but also by means of form discussions, debates, dramatic readings or presentations, while oral composition among the juniors offers valuable opportunities. There should be some reading aloud on the part of the teacher, and his reading should serve as a model; he should make every effort to read clearly, naturally, and in sympathy with his subject-matter, shunning stilted, affected, or artificial methods.

The following are individual opinions:

"'Lectures' by the boys, with insistence on perfect distinctness, or occasional readings to which the rest of the class listen without books, do much to correct faults of slurring, dropping final consonants, and so on. I dislike any methods which concentrate on style and manner without regard to the matter, as leading to the stagey and pedantic speech of the ordinary 'elocutionist.' The boy must have a definite aim before him, namely, to express adequately the meaning (including the emotional tone) of what he reads. Therefore, choose good poetry for him, and teach clear speech, variation of pitch, pace, and expression, incidentally and as a means to that end."

"The reciting of prose does more to promote good speaking than does the reciting of verse. The memorising and reciting of selected prose passages draws attention to the rhythm of the various models of English sentences."

Phonetics

Having regard to the commendation of phonetics by the Departmental Committee, it was desirable to make as definite a recommendation as possible on this point. At present, however, the body of experience is insufficient to justify any detailed advice. Among the supporters of phonetics in English teaching some are strongly of the opinion that it is important for phonetics to begin very early if the value is to be great; others are equally sure that phonetics, and particularly the use of phonetic script, should be postponed till the age of 13. The great majority of the members of the Committee were inclined to think that in most Secondary Schools difficulties of pronunciation could be overcome without any elaborate machinery of phonetics. It is agreed, however, that it is most desirable for teachers of English themselves to have some training in phonetics, so that faults of pronunciation may be corrected systematically and scientifically, while individual teachers must judge how far it is possible and desirable to use phonetic methods in teaching. In short, some very wise words recently written by Mr George Sampson fairly represent the conclusion reached on the subject. "The most valuable result a teacher gets from taking a course in phonetics is not the ability to pass on instruction to a class, but the training of his own ear to distinguish sounds."

Behind the question of good elocution and the use of phonetics is another, that of standard English speech. There is a dread among some members that southern English speech may be taken as a standard if phonetic methods are generally adopted, and they urge very strongly that nothing should be done to inculcate a method of speaking different from the cultured speech of the pupil's own town or district, and this view meets with general support.

CHAPTER II

THE TEACHING OF GRAMMAR

While for the sake of convenience the subject is treated under separate headings, it must never be forgotten that the various branches of English teaching are but means to a single end, and that an attempt to regard the writing of English, for instance, as something which can be isolated from the reading and appreciation of English literature is a mistake and will lead to disaster.

The Case for Grammar Teaching

It is unanimously agreed that from the earliest stages of the Secondary School course some training in formal grammar is necessary and desirable. Without it, it is hardly possible to promote clear thought about the purpose and structure of language or to expect clear expression. To take but one example: those who have had to read illiterate English will find nothing commoner than subjects without predicates or predicates without subjects; only through grammatical teaching can the enormity of this be realised. There is, it is true, a difference of opinion between those teachers who regard grammar as a useful training in clear thinking, and therefore valuable in itself, and those who regard it as a means to an end, a useful servant if nothing more. There is, however, no difference as to its usefulness, and any teacher who has tried to improve the writing of English among people who have had no training at all in grammar will understand and appreciate this point. The writing of English can be taught without a knowledge of grammar, but at the expense of much patience and energy. Remember the girl who tried to show Kipps the difference between "as" and "has."

The fact that grammar has been abused in the past by being made the instrument of the dullest mechanical drudgery— there are still people who claim to have parsed their way through Book 1 of *Paradise Lost*—does not detract from its real value if rightly used. We admit that even to-day in our Secondary Schools there is much mechanical work done in the name of grammar which is deadening—an enemy of all true progress in education. The treatment of grammar purely as a sort of mental gymnastic should be sternly discouraged.

In this respect we take our stand with the Departmental Report and urge concentration on the vital and essential points of grammar, those common to all languages and without which neither the structure of sentences nor the functions of words can be apprehended.

Under the age of 11

The unit of language is the sentence, not the word, and it is only by considering, first, the structure of a sentence that the functions of the constituent words will be understood. The first step, then, will be the consideration of an easy simple sentence and its division into subject and predicate. Dealing with the subject separately will naturally disclose the function of the noun, pronoun, and adjective, just as an examination of the predicate will involve an understanding of the verb and adverb.

From this beginning, if a large variety of sentences be taken, a boy, by eleven, should have an elementary knowledge of the structure of any ordinary simple sentence, including inversions, and of such conceptions as person, number, inflexion, case, voice, the difference between the indicative and the imperative mood, and tense.

If some other language is being learnt at the same time, parallel examples should be taken in it, for the sake of illustration and contrast. It is most important for boys to grasp the fact that all civilised people have the same problems to solve in their languages, that often they solve them in the same way, but that sometimes they do not.

It is extremely valuable that any form of analysis that is adopted should be one which can be used higher in the school, so that a form which can be elaborated easily and logically is to be recommended.

There are several text-books published which set out a course along the lines recommended, but at this stage, except for exercises, which save time and energy, a book is hardly necessary. The work done should be mainly oral, though some time should be devoted to written work from the very beginning. As the pupil grows older the time for written work may be increased.

The thing that should be avoided is acquiescence in mechanical methods—describing English nouns as of neuter gender, for example. Again, definitions should never be given first; if used at all they should be the summary of the child's own experience.

NOTE. Some teachers prefer not to limit themselves at this stage to the simple sentence; there is no reason why the complex sentence should not be handled, provided it is treated as a simple sentence; in fact there are many advantages in accustoming boys early to the idea that groups of words can function as nouns, adjectives, or adverbs.

Throughout the grammar teaching, the Terminology suggested by the Joint Committee, and endorsed by the Departmental Committee, is recommended, though certain criticisms are set forth in an Appendix to this Memorandum.

Suggested forms of analysis:

A. (1) For beginners:

	Subject	Predicate
Sentence		

(2) For more advanced pupils:

		Predicate			
Sentence	Subject*	verb	limitation of verb	object*	complement

* Subject word and object word can be underlined if it is desired.

Or

B. His faithful servants brought him his son home alive:

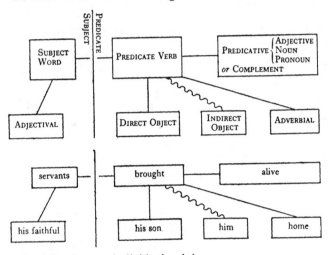

The following are individual opinions:

" I am strongly in favour of a certain amount of formal grammar as a necessary basis for language study. My own syllabus makes provision for analysis of simple sentences: first, into two divisions —Subject and Predicate—later, distinguishing an object, if the verb is Transitive. Beyond these three divisions I do not go, as I think there is in this all the material necessary for teaching the corresponding functions of Nouns and Verbs, Number, Case, etc. I find that analysis is made much more easy by constant exercise in synthesis, *e.g.*, when children are beginning to learn what is meant by the object of a verb used transitively, a multitude of examples (formed by the class) of sentences with ' boy ' as subject, ' boy ' as object, ' boy ' as part of the predicate, certainly fix on the mind the different functions. In addition to the above, I find that adjectives and adverbs are easily taught as additions to the noun and verb. This is the extent of grammar teaching I would advocate at this stage."

and

" Definitions of the parts of speech should in no case be taught first. A definition should be a statement of the function of a word as discovered by a study of examples, *i.e.*, sentences in which the words occur."

The age 11–13

Most of the grammar work will still be oral, though for reasons already given some written work must be done. Assuming that by the age of 11 a boy has a firm grasp of the analysis of a simple sentence, he can now proceed to that of double and complex sentences. There is no need, usually, for the detailed analysis of separate clauses, it being sufficient that their part in the structure of the sentence should be understood, though it may be profitable, on occasion, to examine the clauses in detail orally; an elliptical clause of degree is a case in point.

Quite early, boys should be accustomed to the notion that a group of words can have the same function as a noun, adjective, or adverb, and that sometimes such a group is a clause. The conception should be exemplified by the expansion of simple sentences, and it is here that we find a natural link between grammar and composition.

The essential matter is the realisation of the function of the words in a sentence. It follows, therefore, that the expression of this function, orally or in writing, has a definite value.

Parsing of phrases (adverbial, adjectival, etc.) should go side by side with parsing of single words, and so connect parsing with analysis—the two are all too often divorced, and yet are one and the same thing.

Parsing in the old formal mechanical way is waste of time; it is one thing for boys to understand the meaning of voice, mood, etc., and another to spend time in writing out these particulars about every verb in a long sentence.

By the age of 13, in addition to the functions of the parts of speech, the following points should be known:

VERB (*a*) Distinction between Finite and Infinite.

     (*b*) *Finite Verb.* Voice, Mood, Tense, concord with Subject.

     (*c*) *Infinite Verb.* The Infinitive, the Participles, the Gerund, basing the distinction on form and function.

NOUN OR PRONOUN. The important point is the case, and the reason for the case, since it involves clear thinking about the exact function of the word in the sentence. Some teachers also like to note the kind of noun, but all agree that, while the conceptions of gender and number should be understood, it is a waste of time to write the gender and number of English nouns as a matter of course.

From the age 13 onwards

For another year at least the teaching of grammar should be systematic, concerned with the analysis of ordinary sentences of all kinds and outstanding inflexions and points of syntax; the subjunctive mood, its forms and use, probably encountered about the same time in other languages, is the most important of these. More difficult constructions, such as those involving the use of the infinitive and the participles, can be explained, as well as the simpler idioms.

Regarding grammar teaching as very necessary indeed to a proper training in the language, but still subsidiary, most teachers prefer to stop the systematic teaching of grammar about the age of fourteen in order that the time may be given to more valuable aspects of the English teaching. This is not to say that grammar will be completely disregarded; there must be some grammar teaching incidental to any course of reading, while it will naturally arise in the correction of what has been written. Grammar must be used to explain difficult points of syntax, idioms, and those older forms of English which are encountered in literature or have survived into modern times.

We are speaking generally; in the case of particular sets or forms it may be necessary to continue the grammar teaching for at least another year, possibly until the General School Examination. In this case there will be the same general object in view: the revision of what has already been done, and an extension to include the more difficult applications of general principles already laid down. The systematic study of historical grammar should be reserved until after the First School Examination.

CHAPTER III

THE WRITING OF ENGLISH

Spelling

It is not the opinion of the Committee that spelling can take care of itself, or is something which can be neglected. The simple rules for English spelling (*e.g.* the doubling of the consonant when *-ing* is added) should be taught. Some favour dictation, but although this is a valuable exercise in ear-training, concentration, and punctuation, many think its value for teaching spelling slight. The importance of visual impression (*i.e.* writing a word so that a mental image of its appearance will be retained) should be realised. Bad spellers should keep notebooks; indeed one school thinks it worth while to keep a printed list of words frequently misspelt and circulate it from time to time. With young children some kind of spelling match, or of spelling round the class a few minutes before the end of school, promotes keenness.

If a good foundation is laid in the earlier stages, and above all if the boys are trained to regard spelling as important, spelling can be dealt with in the later stages incidentally, and need not make much demand on the time of the class. Dictation for older boys is not recommended.

Methods of Increasing Vocabulary

Nothing can take the place of reading; all other methods must be secondary to this. Such are the constant use of a dictionary—every boy should have an English dictionary for reference in any difficulty; the suggestion of synonyms and antonyms; the filling of blanks; the encouragement of the observation and examination of new words wherever encountered, even, for young boys, those on hoardings or in cinemas.

Other methods which have been found useful with older boys are:

The turning of school-boy slang into correct English.
The paraphrasing of proverbs.

The distinguishing, especially by the construction of sentences containing them, of words likely to be confused.
The connecting up of words of similar origin, *e.g.* table, tablet, tabulate.

In such exercises use should be made of other languages which are being learnt, while boys not learning Latin or Greek may well have their attention called to the commoner roots and be asked to collect words which contain them.

The Correction of Errors in Composition

Individual correction is no doubt the ideal method, but under present conditions it is a counsel of perfection, though one should aim at giving it to particular members of the class. Selective correction (*i.e.* dealing with a particular type of mistake only) is sometimes valuable. With young boys no great stress should be laid upon the correction of mistakes other than those due to carelessness, since the great aim is to encourage imaginative work and fluency of expression.

A generally recognised code of signs used throughout the school for the correction of composition is strongly recommended. This code may be very definite at first, but as the boys grow older it is better to indicate the mistakes more generally.

Under the age of 11

Just as the sentence should be the unit of grammar, so it should be the unit of composition. "A bare outline can be expanded by the addition of phrases and subordinate clauses (without mentioning these names). Emphasis on the sentence as the unit is necessary, as many children on entering the school are unable to distinguish when they have written a complete thought, and so find a great difficulty in punctuation."

While grammar and composition should be correlated so that grammar and composition exercises both bear on the same point, the scope of the composition work will not be restricted to the stage reached in grammar; a boy expressing himself naturally will use more complicated constructions than would be dealt with in the grammar teaching.

Many teachers prefer to do without a book, but one containing suitable graded exercises will save time and help to keep the work in parallel forms on the same lines. A text-book which relates grammar and composition is recommended, while at this stage, pictures, or series of pictures, should often be used as a basis for composition.

Most of the work in composition should be oral, partly because it is possible in this way to cover much more ground, and achieve much greater variety, and partly because it promotes careful speech and expression. There is, too, the sense of co-operative effort, for many a young boy who could not manage a complete composition by himself will be ready and anxious to add his contribution. At the same time, it is the writing of English that we are aiming at, and, from the first, some time each week should be devoted to written work, increasing as the boy gains confidence and skill.

The following are examples of exercises which have been recommended:

(a) *Reproductive*.
> Re-telling a story.
> Elaborating an outline.

(b) *Imaginative*.
> Writing a letter.
> Finishing a story partly told.
> Dialogue.
> Stories to illustrate proverbs.
> Writing the autobiography of an animal or of some object.
> Writing on some subject chosen by the child.
> The dramatisation of some ballad such as Robin Hood.
> (The writing of verse is not recommended, though many regard it as useful for gaining a sense of rhythm, and a training in the choice of words.)

(c) *Descriptive*.
> Framing simple sentences round some object and combining them.
> Account of a game or walk.
> Description of a picture or poster.
> Writing out descriptions of experiments, directions for reaching a place, or recipes for making things.

Apart from these examples, valuable exercises in synthesis, in word association (*e.g.* fitting appropriate adjectives to nouns), in the construction of similes, can be used, though they lend themselves to oral rather than written work.

In written compositions it is a most useful plan to insist upon five minutes being spent in reading over the work and correcting faults before the work is handed in.

Types of exercises which are not suitable for young boys are: the correction of faulty sentences, for boys may thus be introduced to mistakes which would otherwise never occur to them; paraphrase; the turning of direct into indirect speech; the sequence of tenses.

A record of actual experience follows:

"I depend mainly upon reading. Each week an extract which has been carefully selected for appeal and interest is read aloud to the class. Upon this the week's exercises are based. These are grouped under the following heads:

> (i) Word-study.
> (ii) Sentence-making.
> (iii) Punctuation.
> (iv) The choice of words.
> (v) Constructive work.

That is, the pupil, under the master's guidance, first pulls a selected example of literary craftsmanship to pieces to see what it is made of. He observes new words and familiar words in fresh settings. He learns how to combine them to express ideas, and then how to point them, so that one does not run indiscriminately into the next. He notices, too, that *any* word will not do, and his observations under this heading will constitute his first lessons in literary style.

Having done this pulling to pieces he will naturally wish to reverse the process and do some constructive work on his own account. So by being set to write on subjects that arise out of the reading-matter he has been examining, he exercises this constructive faculty. The subjects and forms must be as varied as possible. The aim at this stage will not be technical ability, but interest and expression."

The age 11–13

The work should proceed upon the lines already laid down; some of it must be oral, and the exercises of the same general type already suggested. A valuable practice is to get a member of a class to give an account of some manual work (*e.g.* how to mend a puncture) and invite criticism by other boys. Sentence building on a selected series of words and the reproduction of stories are other obvious exercises. In connection with the latter it adds variety and interest to re-tell the story from another point of view, *e.g.* Lord Ullin describes the fate of his daughter. Re-telling a tale in another form (turning narrative into dialogue), for example, is an exercise of a similar kind and value.

The composing of brief, accurate definitions of simple objects. *e.g.* a chair, a cupboard, a tile, is another suitable exercise, The results should be compared with those of a good dictionary. Such work encourages close thinking and condensed expression.

Side by side with the oral work should be a fair amount of written work, consisting partly of exercises and partly of complete compositions. A well-chosen book will save much time in the construction and dictation of suitable exercises, while the written compositions will be largely based on the oral work already done on the same subject. The practice at this stage of always discussing the matter before a composition is written is to be deprecated. At all stages there should be an opportunity for imagination and originality. Letter writing may well play an important part, and the boy should be ready to write short descriptive compositions or short biographies.

Among the exercises the combining of sentences into paragraphs should hold an important place; just as the concentration at an early stage should be on the sentence, so here it should be on the paragraph. In this connection some instruction in punctuation must be given, and the use of the full stop, the comma, and the semi-colon understood. If clear rules are given, bad punctuation can be returned for correction by reference to these rules.

Apart from the general remarks already made on the subject of correction, it is agreed that boys should be taught to correct more for themselves as they grow older; if the plan of a definite set of symbols for mistakes has been adopted, the boy knows the kind of mistake he has made and can correct it without further assistance. A few go so far as to deny this help, and merely indicate a mistake, but the general opinion is against this.

Generally speaking, style should receive more attention than at an earlier stage; for instance, selected ugly sentences can be read out and re-cast in class. This can be done without allowing superficial faults of handwriting and spelling to pass without notice. A good working plan is to give positive marks for matter, arrangement, style, etc., but to deduct marks for those other faults which come largely from carelessness. Where sufficient time is at the teacher's disposal it is often the rule to insist upon a fair copy of the composition. At least sentences embodying corrections should be re-written.

The question of verse composition revealed an interesting diversity of experience, for while some members have found it extremely valuable, others have tried it with little success. Those who have found it successful have generally found, also, that younger children do better than those of this age. The weight of experience shows that there is much to be said in favour of verse composition as an occasional exercise; it will help to train the ear, and it will enforce attention to the rhythm of verse. "A boy who has himself tried to write a stanza in ballad metre will have a much greater appreciation of the music of a ballad than one who has never tried." The class should have a clear idea of the particular form in which they are asked to write before attempting it, and those who show no aptitude should have an alternative exercise set.

The exercise of putting verse into prose form and asking the class to put it back into metrical form serves no useful purpose; nor, at this stage, does the setting of imitative work, for example, the writing of some sentences in the style of Stevenson or Dickens.

The age 13–16

A. The Essay.

Some careful system of grading should be worked out so that there may be progression. This seems a truism, but there are still schools where boys of fourteen are expected to write on a purely abstract theme. The grading can be obtained by beginning with purely descriptive essays, varied by autobiographical subjects—"What I should do if..."; thence to essays making some demand on the critical faculties, such as "My favourite novel"; and finally to philosophical subjects needing the marshalling of arguments pro and con. A very similar line of approach will be from paragraph work, by means of narrative essays and descriptions, to the critical essay. It should be unnecessary to set a boy of thirteen reproductive compositions, unless there is also a change of form, e.g. from the narrative to dialogue, from the direct to the indirect, or giving a much condensed account of a longer narrative—all of them valuable exercises, especially in the earlier stages. Whatever grading by subject is adopted, there should also be progression as regards length and treatment, so that no one kind of essay should be completely discarded as the boy grows older; there should at all times be some variety in the subjects chosen as themes. The pupil himself should generally be allowed a certain amount of choice; some teachers go so far as to allow the suggestion of subjects with, of course, the right of veto by the teacher.

The practice of setting a regular weekly essay on some formal subject is, in the opinion of the Committee, wrong; one set some time previously and at more infrequent intervals, and carefully corrected, is of far more use. Several advocate the careful thinking out of a list of essays for the term and the giving of the list to the form in advance. Of course there will be written work in the interval—the use of subsidiary exercises in vocabulary, the preparation of skeleton essays, letter writing, and so on. Oral work should not be neglected at any stage, though naturally there will be less of it as the boys grow older. It is desirable at all stages to work over the ground of an essay in class occasionally before the essay is written. No method, however, should prevent the free play of imagination, or tend to cramp individual ways of approaching and handling the subject. In considering oral work we must never forget the importance of discussion, whether in formal debates or in informal talks. Very experienced teachers have found that, where debates were a decided failure, the delivery of short explanations or lectures by members of the form, followed by criticism on the part of others, are most profitable. The subjects for such explanations had better be quite concrete and definite—the description of a piece of machinery, directions for reaching a certain place, and the like. The object should be to promote clear thinking and clear expression.

Anything which brings a touch of novelty or reality into the work should be welcomed; for example, insisting sometimes that letters should be written on note-paper and put into addressed envelopes, the construction of dialogues between a Rugby player and an Association player. One member puts in a valuable caution against the type of dialogue where there is no real point of contact between the speakers—Queen Elizabeth and the Wife of Bath, for instance.

On the question of correction it is agreed that the more

individual correction the better; in special cases it may be necessary to see particular boys after the lesson. Time being limited, there must in practice be much collective treatment, a summary of the chief good points noticed in the whole batch, a condemnation of the chief faults. A good essay may be read with stress on its merits and suggestions *passim* for improvement; a bad essay should not be read in its entirety, though extracts may be dealt with both by the other boys and the master. The use of a code is still recommended, but while for the younger boys it may be fairly complete, it should gradually become less elaborate. Long notes by the teacher in the margin or at the end are of little use; it is necessary that the boys themselves should correct what is wrong; sentences, passages, and even whole essays should be re-written.

Where numerical marks are given it is well to have some scheme, not too cast-iron, but intelligible—a proportion for matter and arrangement, another proportion for form and style, with marks deducted for bad writing, spelling, and punctuation. Merit symbols are much more satisfactory, though here it is better to give a double set, one for matter and arrangement, another for form and style.

An experiment which has proved successful is to make each boy write an occasional essay each term in a special book which is kept, throughout his career, as a test of progress—not necessarily a picked essay, but one written without any preliminary talk or preparation by the teacher. A large number of teachers encourage effort by putting promising essays into the form magazine, or into a special collection of writings in prose or verse.

B. Précis Writing.

The following opinions on the value and method of précis writing are endorsed by the Revising Committee. They give the opinion of that Committee from slightly varying points of view:

Its Value.

(1) Précis writing is of great educational value in that it strengthens the intellect in its power to select with sound judgment, to appreciate logical and balanced argument and arrangement, to view the whole and shape it into a unity; and in that it forms and improves the taste in the corresponding

matters of style in appreciation. The resulting power to write a well expressed, well co-ordinated, coherent, and homogeneous piece of English prose is invaluable.

But précis writing has too often been considered as an exercise apart. This may be due to its special place in Civil Service and other examinations, in which the common form of a series of letters or other documents, minutes of evidence, reports of business meetings, etc., often of no particular literary value, has tended to mark out the exercise as distinct from literature, if not merely as a matter of technical skill. The careful study of the better kinds of passages set forth for précis is education in literary appreciation, and much careful study is essential to the writing of a good précis.

(2) There is a somewhat widespread notion that précis writing is an exercise the final value of which concerns the business house, the daily newspaper and the Government office; that is, its value is purely commercial or, at any rate, vocational.

Such a notion minimises seriously, even if it does not caricature, one of the fundamental processes involved in all true mental progress—the process, namely, either of distinguishing between essentials and unessentials in thought, or of grasping the true relationship of ideas which, though all pertinent to the issue, are nevertheless of varying importance. This process calls for intellectual effort and affects all phases of human thought,—literature, science, politics, religion, philosophy and so on; and it is this intellectual effort that précis writing, properly taught, should initiate and develop. To be such a mental instrument, however, précis writing should be associated only very occasionally with such vocational exercises as commercial correspondence, minutes of evidence and journalistic reports. Its exercises should be drawn from the best that our language has to give in the way of writings and speeches on literature, art, music, science, history, politics, and even religion and philosophy. Granted such exercises, précis writing would afford a much-needed training in mental discrimination and judgment, and in clearness and precision in speech and writing. But it would do much more than this, for, by its instruction in cultured knowledge, and by the discussion and comment to which such exercises should give rise under a capable teacher, it could and should quite naturally lead to creative thought of a determinate value rarely attainable with certainty in even the best essay writing.

Method.

Précis writing may well begin, by way of summaries of work read and of work written, in low forms—*e g.* ages 11–13. It is important to have very brief summaries in the lowest forms and to increase the length and the attention to exact detail as the work goes up the school. Précis for young boys is only an extension of what they always have to do orally, viz.: to answer questions on what they have just read; *e.g.* "What did Jim overhear when he was in the apple barrel?" In the year 14–15 the more careful précis should be begun: it should not be left to the year of the First School Examination. Experience shows that boys are "lost" if they begin the writing of précis only in the examination year. Passages should be set for précis from prose, poetry, and the drama, and on a variety of subjects and in a variety of styles. Narrative and dialogue may be set first, then description, and by the year 15–16 boys will be able to manage exposition and argument. Series of letters, telegrams, etc., can be begun as early as 13–14. It is a useful exercise for a boy to write an analysis and a précis of his own essay.

Stages in working out a précis:

(1) The first reading, which will give the general idea, and perhaps, the title.

(2) A careful study of the passage, very much on the lines of the *lecture expliquée*. Consideration of such matters as vocabulary (*e.g.* synonyms), relation of ideas, construction of sentences, characteristics of style, relative importance of details (*e.g.* essential or merely illustrative).

(3) A plan or analysis of the passage. This will be sometimes by way of main headings, sub-headings, and perhaps further subordination; sometimes by more graphic devices. This stage is invaluable for selection of essential facts and for ensuring arrangement and proportion in the précis.

(4) A first draft of the précis can now be made without reference to the original, or even without reference to the analysis. With increasing skill less and less revision will be necessary.

(5) The final précis, for which, as a rule, condensation is the chief need. This may involve some further omissions of less important details, recasting of sentences, clearly implying ideas instead of expressing them explicitly, replacing clauses by phrases and phrases by single words, and perhaps some regrouping—all to the end of a good and polished piece of prose of the required length.

(6) The Title.

The following are individual opinions:

" In an informal way, this exercise is always a part of English teaching. It begins with the re-telling of a verse or prose story in the pupils' own words, and develops in the statement of the main ideas of a paragraph or series of paragraphs of the prose non-fiction reader. Its value as an exercise in understanding and expression is obvious. If pupils have been well trained in this *oral précis* (without the terrifying name) they will find it easy to pass to the written form.

This should begin with the written summary of an easy paragraph, and the framing of a title, and continue with passages of graduated difficulty. It may be profitably combined with indirect speech. The aim of the oral exercise—concentration on meaning and its expression in the pupils' *own* words—must be kept clearly in sight. Many teachers recommend the making of rough notes on the meaning of the passage. When satisfied that these notes represent the true meaning, the pupils then express them in connected form without reference to the original, to avoid its phrasing. Parallel with the précis of a complete passage, the condensation of verbose sentences is a valuable exercise in attaining a brevity which can be accurately tested. Although we do not consider the précis as important as the essay, since the expression of original ideas is more important than reproduction, the value of précis in concentration, clear thinking, and concise expression cannot be too highly emphasised."

"I am fully convinced now that it is most necessary that précis should be dealt with as a definite topic in the English course, almost from the earliest stages. Formerly I was of the opinion that boys would 'pick up' the art of précis instinctively from their study of a text-book subject such as history, and that a mere incidental treatment was all that the English teacher need give. Now I treat it as it arises incidentally, *e.g.*, in the course of reading a play or novel ample opportunity is afforded for the condensation of arguments, and also as a piece of independent work, using passages such as those included in

Low and Briggs's *Matriculation English*, or Morgan and Treble's *English Composition*. The making of a précis of correspondence I have also found useful to boys when they leave school, though here the finding of material is somewhat difficult. As to method adopted, I follow that advocated in the Low and Briggs book mentioned above."

"I hold that the précis, especially when in indirect form, is a most searching test of a boy's power of clear thinking and expression. By compelling a close examination of language, it develops the critical faculty. I find that it tends to correct loose expression and sloppiness of style. The essayist is certainly the better for his training in précis work."

"I do not think that précis can be taught at all as a separate branch, without squeezing out more necessary literature. For this reason I can teach it as a distinct branch only in one form (age 15–16), with a commercial bias—a form that has extra time for English."

"I consider précis important—by précis, however, I mean not 'commercial' or 'civil service' précis, but I think boys should be able to give a brief résumé of a book they have studied or read; practice in this kind of thing gives a habit of mentally arranging one's reading round a framework—a faculty very valuable later on when progress depends in many cases on wide reading and the assimilation of ideas."

"My idea of précis writing is that it is vitally important both in the reading and the writing of English. It is the finest method of testing a pupil's ability to understand a passage, and further, it tests his ability to express his thoughts in terse language. Arrangement, so important in the essay, is here all important. Every word counts. It is an antidote to 'padding,' so common an evil in essay writing."

C. Other Exercises in Writing.

1. **Paraphrase.** Many teachers are very doubtful as to the value of paraphrasing poetry as a written exercise. They feel that its purpose and intention may so easily be misunderstood both by the boys and by outside examining bodies; the former may easily persuade themselves that their prose versions are in some way superior to the original. Again it concentrates attention on the meaning of the words in a narrow sense, and makes the readers ignore the beauty of rhythm and sound. Yet its value as a test of understanding, and as a means of expressing the ideas and feelings aroused by the poetry, can hardly be overlooked. It is agreed that the paraphrase of

archaic or diffuse prose is often a valuable exercise, that a considerable amount of oral paraphrase incidentally in the course of reading is necessary. The poetry should not be chosen from the greatest and noblest passages, it should not be so simple that paraphrase is the merest juggling with words (*e.g.* Drayton's *Agincourt*) or so difficult that the majority of the class get no credit because they have failed to understand the original.

2. **Correction of Faulty English.** The recasting of sentences and correction of errors in grammar, order of words, and choice of words have been found of value at this stage.

3. **The Imitative Essay.** Very few advocate the use of this before the age of 16. For older boys and a few exceptionally imaginative boys it has a value, but the rest will seize on a few mannerisms and miss the essential points. One correspondent, however, has been successful in getting his pupils to follow the method of treating the subject as distinct from the style of writing; another member calls special attention to the title as showing how a subject, which to a boy seems quite unpromising, can be handled by a great writer.

4. **Verse Writing.** With certain limitations and reservations this has proved extremely valuable; in a few exceptional cases it may develop a genuine poetic faculty, but this is not the main reason for its recommendation; indeed there is a danger, which must be guarded against, that precocious efforts may be over-rated, and the Committee deprecates the publication, except in school magazines, of efforts which show facility or even promise. Its value lies rather in the lessons in appreciation which it promotes. Then, exercises should never be too long, a stanza or two, a few couplets or so to enforce attention to the laws of prosody. Since some boys are incapable of writing even this amount, an alternative should usually be provided, *i.e.*, it seems best to make verse composition voluntary. A good plan is to read the verses in class and invite criticism, after which the verse which by common consent is the best is entered into a special book, or put aside for the form magazine.

Parody arouses interest; one member has described a most amusing one, in the style of the *Faerie Queene*, on a modern subject, while another has an engaging description of a school worthy copied from Chaucer's *Prologue*.

Two particular exercises seem worthy of recommendation. One is the setting of verses with certain words omitted, the class being asked to supply those words, comparing the results with the original. The second is the reading of the substance of a stanza, in simple prose, which the pupils thereupon turn into verse; here, too, the results should be compared with the original.

D. The application of the Reading of Literature to the Teaching of Writing.

All agree that only by reading much will boys become good writers, but the effect must be largely indirect. Just as the old-fashioned teacher regarded what was read as a medium for practice in analysis or parsing, or for the teaching of etymology, so there is a danger that we may use it too consciously as a model for writing. The unconscious influence of reading good models must be reinforced at all stages by the memorising of good prose as well as of poetry. Yet there are many direct methods by which literature ought to be used to promote good writing. The occasional dissection of a well-balanced sentence, the comparison of sentences of different structure, the contrasting of Bacon and Lamb as regards methods and expression, are instances.

In many ways the literature read should be made to provide material for practice in writing. Examples are the recasting in other forms; the suggestion of alternatives to the development in the original; above all, the writing of some kind of critical appreciation.

An interesting record of personal experience is given:

"The writing of English is based on the study of suitable models. In the first stage of the period of school life now under review, narratives of a stirring character will be read (*e.g.* Lytton's *Death of Harold*) as well as vivid descriptive passages (*e.g.* Ruskin's *Slave Ship* or Byron's *Falls of Terni*). Later, work of a quieter and more meditative character will gradually be introduced. The boys will learn to *philosophize*, as Sir Arthur Quiller-Couch puts it.

The oral work will include the usual debates, impromptu speeches and lectures prepared beforehand on subjects chosen by the pupils themselves; these last to be followed by intervals for questions and discussion. This work may be co-ordinated with the written work by selecting certain members of the class to report the proceedings, the reports themselves to be read at the next meeting and to form the subject of further discussion.

The written work will roughly fall into the following stages:

13–14. Informal sketches, short stories.

14–15. The same, gradually merging into more formal discussions.

15–16. The essay proper. (Not neglecting the previous stages, of course.)

In correction distinctive marks should be employed for certain easily recognised types of errors. For example:

A. Mistakes in 'agreement.'

R. Needless repetition.

P. Error in punctuation.

S. Error in spelling.

This can provide the basis of useful work in class, when common errors can be discussed and corrected.

Paraphrase is found very useful, but only when done on freer lines than is often allowed. Insistence upon an exact equivalent is likely to do more harm than good. If we may take the analogy of translating from a foreign language, what is wanted is a free rendering that preserves the spirit and atmosphere of the original rather than a literal translation.

Imitative essays are not used.

Verse writing affords good practice within limits. The aim is two-fold:

(i) To give some practical knowledge of versification.

(ii) To give some appreciation of the difficulty of the poet's task.

The aim is not to produce a certain amount of machine-made verse."

The following is another record:

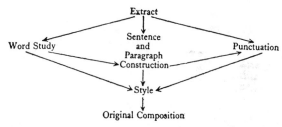

"The above diagram will give an indication of the plan by which an attempt is made to use literature in teaching the writing of English.

The whole is based on a series of carefully chosen graded selections which are studied intensively. These are so chosen as to give from first to last an idea of the range of our literature and of the wealth of its forms.

The pupil is taken, as it were, into the writer's workshop, and sees there how he uses his raw material, *i.e.* words. Then he notes how these words are combined and related, and so the word-study passes into sentence-construction and the formation of the paragraph. This in turn leads naturally to punctuation as the method by which sentences and phrases are separated. The pupil will not go far, however, before he discovers that a writer has characteristic ways of employing his material that mark him out from all other craftsmen. This is what we know as style, and on this all the exercises of word-study, sentence-construction and punctuation converge. Having done so much, the pupil will naturally want to work on his own account, and suggestive composition exercises arising out of the work studied will enable him to try his hand."

CHAPTER IV

THE READING AND APPRECIATION OF ENGLISH

General Remarks

1. **Anthologies.** Whatever else is read, every pupil should have a carefully chosen anthology which should be the foundation on which the work is based. Some prefer an anthology which can be carried through the school, but generally it is better to have three anthologies, or one in three grades, lower, middle, and upper. A good plan that is practicable in some cases is for the school itself to make its own anthology; where this is done in manuscript it is not always easy to keep the notebooks clean and in good condition.

The use of an anthology need not exclude the occasional reading of long poems where time permits.

2. **Reading aloud by the Teacher.** Since good poems are often spoilt by the bad way in which they are read for the first time, and since the impression made is not seldom a lasting one,

it is generally desirable that the first reading of a fresh poem should be by the teacher. Further, a good reading will reveal unsuspected beauties, and stimulate the appreciation of poems previously read. In the early stages, particularly, the teacher himself should read frequently, but two considerations must never be lost sight of: first, the real danger that the teacher's pleasure in reading may lead him to monopolise the time available; second, that the manner in which a child reads, especially something fresh, is a most valuable indication of progress in appreciation.

3. **The Manner of Reading Aloud.** Reading should be natural, but great pains should be taken with it, so that tone, pitch, and pace are suitable to the subject-matter. By "natural" should be understood the avoidance of the conversational on the one hand, and of a stilted artificial style on the other. With young boys it may be necessary to emphasise rhythm and rhyme; certainly these should be clearly brought out.

4. **Silent Reading in School.** This is valuable if time allows; the real difficulty is the checking of what is done, as otherwise the value is to a large extent lost. Several teachers keep special "rapid readers" on hand for use, partly at home, partly at school. Discussions in class are the most satisfactory way of securing interest, and ensuring, too, that a real effort is made to read.

5. **Repetition and the Choice of Passages.** There are many reasons why repetition should not be dropped: the most important is that the passages learnt form a background of good literature which will be a permanent possession of lasting value. Repetition promotes good articulation, good pronunciation, and in some cases self-possession. It does not train the memory for other purposes.

Within limits, the choice may be made by the pupils themselves. Some passages should be selected by the teacher himself to ensure that the best passages are not omitted, the rest being taken from a number approved by him. If the anthology used is suitable, the choice will naturally be made from it. The anthology built up in school may be confined to the passages learnt by heart, so that there may be opportunities for revision in the higher parts of the school.

6. **The Teaching of Prosody.** There should be no formal attempt in the junior forms to teach the principles of prosody, but even in these forms attention should be directed to the importance of rhythm and beat. The ear should also be trained to recognise good and bad rhyme. Many teachers believe that technical terms may be safely used even with young boys.

Between the ages of 14 and 15 a boy should have a sufficient grasp of the technology of prosody to enable him to understand thoroughly the structure of the poetry he is reading. This will be best obtained by constant study of the prosody of the poems, and by imitative verse writing.

The following are individual opinions:

"I have recently become more and more convinced that the best appreciation comes through attempted imitation. Thus, one of my colleagues has recently achieved marked success in teaching prosody to a 'Transitus' form by getting them to write sonnets. Last year I treated the ballad form in the same way with the same set of boys with gratifying results."

"Attention to the more irregular rhythm of prose, side by side with the regular rhythm of verse, is of great help in training boys to read aloud."

7. **Methods of Promoting and Testing Understanding.** Passages should be studied in such a way that the pupil can:

(*a*) enumerate the points made in description or argument;

(*b*) observe and explain peculiar words and expressions;

(*c*) note the use made of figures of speech;

(*d*) observe the punctuation, sentence construction and order of words, if they call for special attention.

It is a useful practice, after the first careful reading of a book, to get the form, working in conjunction with the master, to draw up a list of questions dealing with important aspects of the work as they have revealed themselves. A selection of these may be answered, either in note form or as essays, while the work is being studied in detail.

8. **Methods of Promoting and Testing Appreciation.** On no point is there a greater variety of opinion than on this. Many doubt whether in the early stages much can be done to test literary appreciation at all, or whether it is really desirable to attempt it in any formal way. If the work done is suitable

in material and in method, and above all, if the personality of the teacher is what it should be, then good results will follow, but it will hardly be possible to test them until a later stage.

We must remember that, in expressing opinions, children will often say not what they think but what is likely to meet with approval. At the same time talks about the books read must be the chief means of judging the progress made. Form magazines, too, are not without value.

Adverse criticism of books popular among the children should be used sparingly, but there is no reason why comparison between the good and bad should not be made occasionally (*e.g.* the *Jungle Books* and *Tarzan*). A book should never be condemned without good reasons being given.

Some records of personal experience are quoted:

"Training in appreciation should be mainly incidental, and taken in a matter-of-fact way. Gush and insincerity are fatal. Start from the basic fact that tastes differ, and if a boy does not respond to what delights you, do not put him down as a Philistine.

We can encourage appreciation by avoiding sham reverence, and promoting frankness between the class and the teacher. If the class, by a large majority, after discussion, vote Mr Pickwick silly and dull, then our blackboard criticism shall say so. Gently one would insinuate reasons for thinking differently; but the class opinion *is* the class opinion. In point of fact, the class generally is pretty just. When they see that their opinions count, they take great interest in forming them, and defend their favourites against attacks.

Good reading by the teacher means a sure road to appreciation by those temperamentally fitted to appreciate the particular piece in question.

Before the boys can appreciate literature the teacher must first do so. In no other sort of teaching does the personality of the teacher count for so much. The teacher of literature must be able to communicate his enthusiasm to the class. If the class know that he is reading a poem for the twentieth time and enjoying it more than ever, they will be bound to catch some of his enthusiasm.

May I quote, to show the need of the teacher's reading aloud, an experience of my own with an Evening Class in English—artisans of 19–20 years of age. During a discussion on books on the opening night of the session, several explained that books recommended as good they had found to be lacking in interest and excitement. I read to them the scene in the inn from *The Cloister and the Hearth*. Several had already read the novel, and one naïvely summed up the opinion of the rest—'We didn't find anything as exciting as that.' This incident brought home to me the fact that much silent reading is ineffective.

I am a believer in the dictum—'Always read poetry twice—the first time for the sound, the second for the sense.' I always find that unless the rhyme and rhythm are well marked in my reading, the boys fail to grow enthusiastic."

9. **The Control of Private Reading.** While actual control is seldom practicable or even desirable, some attempt should be made to *guide* the boys' private reading.

The following methods have been found successful:

> Providing lists of books, establishing a Form Library, the set reading of one book a term out of school, discussions on books, making books the subject for compositions, co-operation with the public library of the town or district, drawing attention to accounts of current events and matters of literary interest in good newspapers and periodicals.

The setting of books to be read in the holidays, though very common, has not been found of value in practice, for the books are rarely read except at the very last moment.

There are several ways in which the Form Library can be established. One method is the purchase of one volume by each boy, the books bought having the approval of the master, and then fortnightly exchanges, the original purchaser reclaiming his own book at the end of the term or session; another is for the master in the first place to buy all the books, and each of the boys to obtain a book from him, preference being given by place in form or by lot.

Under the age of 11

1. **The kind of Poetry to be Read.** The great necessity at this stage is for the poetry read to be simple, and, though narrative poetry should predominate, there should be no attempt to confine the reading to it. Children vary in taste, and we should try to make use of this difference and direct it. Lyrical poetry in particular often appeals to young boys, who are sometimes highly imaginative.

Among the kinds of poetry recommended as suitable, apart from purely narrative poetry, are:

> Lyrical poetry (including Shakespeare's songs), Nature poetry, Ballads, Patriotic poetry, Descriptive poetry, Fairy poetry, Humorous poetry.

The extracts or poems to be learnt at this stage should never be too long, *e.g.* the whole of the *Ancient Mariner*, and, with the exception of passages from the Authorised Version of the Bible, should be confined to poetry.

2. **Single Poems for Young Children.** The great variety of single poems mentioned as successful proves how much children vary in taste; generally speaking, they prefer a poem with a "good galloping metre." Among the typical poems which found favour were the following:

Galloping metre	*How They Brought the Good News.*
Nature ...	Wordsworth's *Daffodils.*
	Tennyson's *Brook.* (Not the narrative part of the poem.)
Humorous ...	*John Gilpin.*
Fairy ...	*The Pied Piper.*
Ballad ...	*Sir Patrick Spens.*
Patriotic ...	*The Spanish Armada.*
Songs ...	*Under the Greenwood Tree.*
Miscellaneous	*King Robert of Sicily.*
	Newbolt's *He Fell among Thieves.*
	De la Mare's *Nod.*
	Bab Ballads—*The Yarn of The Nancy Bell.*
	Drinkwater's *Mamble.*

3. **Drama.** While the classic drama is not suitable in its entirety for children of this age, selected scenes may be read with advantage. Reading from the drama should be confined to plays arranged from ballads or such a book as *Alice in Wonderland*. Such plays are often constructed by the children themselves, and those in Dent's *Junior Form-Room Plays* are recommended as showing the kind of play to be read.

Such reading should be associated with some acting, preferably in costume. Many have found that this does not demand so much time as might be expected, and that it adds a reality to the work, and claims an interest which would otherwise be lost. Part-reading, *i.e.* reading allotted parts on the platform or classroom floor in front of the form, is a compromise not to be despised where time is very limited. Drama should always be read as drama, never as an involved kind of story.

It follows that there must be some attempt at simple analysis of character and plot to enable the children to realise their parts. The analysis, then, will be incidental to the reading and acting, not a formal thing apart from the main current of the work.

4. **Prose Reading.** The view was put forward that at this stage all the reading should be confined to poetry on the ground that the children would read prose for themselves, and that appreciation is best fostered by means of poetry. This opinion is not endorsed, because many children do not read good prose for themselves, and exclusive reading of poetry will lead to the impression that prose is not literature and that literature has little connection with every-day life. At least there must be, even at this stage, some introduction to the great prose writers. Complete prose texts, extracts, abridgments, all have their advantages and their drawbacks. If complete prose texts are used, they must be short and the reading should never be carried on from one term to another. The *Christmas Carol* is an instance of a suitable prose text. Well-chosen extracts are probably the most used at this stage: they should be of a fair length and complete in themselves—we must oppose the tendency to snippets. They should be of varying character, generally narrative. As far as possible, the complete text from which the extracts are taken should be accessible to the children, though it is to be doubted whether in most cases the reading of extracts sends the readers to the original book. Abridgments would seem to be a satisfactory compromise, but very few teachers are content with existing abridgments. Probably the best solution, if abridgments are preferred, is for the class to have the complete texts and for the teacher to make his own cuts, leaving the pupils to read what is omitted if they choose. It is often useful, as promoting concentration, for the teacher occasionally to read something of which the pupils have no copies.

The question was raised whether such a book as *Treasure Island* should be read in school, seeing that it would probably be read in any case. It was shown that at home it would be read simply for the story, and its qualities as literature would never be appreciated. Here is an unrivalled opportunity of showing in a simple way how a hackneyed theme can be the basis for a work of genius.

The age 11–13

Where boys join the school between these ages, it is desirable that they should read in some simplified form the body of literature which has already been read by those who entered earlier. Particular care should be taken that they should read something of the stories based on Classic, Teutonic, and Celtic Legend and Myth. Apart from their intrinsic interest and value, so much of our literature assumes a knowledge of these legends that a boy is handicapped unless he has some background of such knowledge. To quote one of our members, speaking of such boys, "The storehouse of ancient legend, myth, and history appears to be almost entirely neglected; in a good form of 20 boys not more than 8 knew anything of the Iliad or the Odyssey, and no one knew who Achilles was."

For such boys, then, the syllabus for the first year should include such books as the *Tanglewood Tales*, Kingsley's *Heroes*, Church's *Stories from Ancient Greece*, and its companion *Stories from Ancient Rome*, Macaulay's *Lays*, and *Tales from the Northern Sagas*.

With this reservation, reading for the year 11–12 should include:

(*a*) A verse anthology, either the one used previously or a more advanced book of the same series. Dent's *Story Poems*, and the Oxford *Book of Verse for Boys and Girls*, Part II, are suggested as illustrative of the standard.

(*b*) Parts of a longer poem, such as *Hiawatha* or *The Lay of the Last Minstrel*.

(*c*) Prose extracts, such as those in *Chips from a Book Shelf* or Elizabeth Lee's *Selections*.

(*d*) Such a collection of easy plays as Dent's *Junior Form-Room Plays*.

The above are for intensive study, and do not exclude other books for rapid reading either at home or at school. Such are *Treasure Island*, *Hereward the Wake*, *The Black Arrow*, *The Talisman*, *The Refugees*. The practice still prevalent in some schools of reading books like these through in class in minute doses is utterly wrong. A preliminary talk to arouse interest and secure background will precede the actual reading. This may be about the author, or about the time when the story is supposed to happen, or any other point which presents itself as suitable. Then occasional lessons in class will ensure that the book is really being read, and will promote appreciation; at the end will come talks and discussions about the book, its plot, the characters, the style, comparison with other books on the same subject, or recently read, and indeed anything which will make the book a real and valued possession of the reader. There are perhaps three dangers: concentration on the *facts* of the story to the exclusion of other points, want of variety in the methods employed, and trying to deal so exhaustively with the book that there is a reaction of boredom.

Similar methods, amplified, will serve in dealing with rapid reading at later stages.

It will be noticed that the reading of complete plays of Shakespeare is not recommended at the age under consideration; indeed the weight of opinion is against doing so before the age of 13, though a number of teachers with wide experience think this can be done between 12 and 13, if such plays as *A Midsummer Night's Dream*, *Henry V*, and *Julius Caesar* are chosen. It must not be forgotten that this difference of opinion does not extend to the reading of many selected scenes; boys should certainly begin to do this by the age of 12.

Closely connected is the question whether Lamb's *Tales* should be read as an introduction to Shakespeare. Most teachers regard the *Tales* as a body of reading intrinsically valuable, and useful as an introduction to the Plays. They urge that for the average boy the pleasure is enhanced and not diminished by knowing already something of the story and of the characters, while the dramatic side can be emphasised by asking the class to dramatise the *Tales* as told by Lamb, for there is sufficient conversation to supply material. (*Lamb and Shakespeare*, Dent, shows how this can be done.) There is, too, the style of the *Tales* to be taken into account. It is worth remembering that it is very usual to read such a play as *The Merchant of Venice* in a simple way at a comparatively early stage, and again more intensively at a later one, and that the value of the later reading is not destroyed by the previous knowledge.

While this is the opinion of most teachers, there are some who strongly disapprove of reading the *Tales* on the ground that they concentrate the attention on the story, and diminish the interest and pleasure called forth by reading the plays with fresh minds. Far, too, from admiring the style, they think it is a bad one for young children to become familiar with.

Reading for the age 12–13 will be:

1. Poems from an anthology.

2. Extracts from some longer poems, such as *The Lady of the Lake* or *Marmion*, or the whole of such a poem as *Mazeppa* or *Sohrab and Rustum*. (The authorities of Rugby School pointed out the popularity of the latter some years ago, and their view is endorsed by general experience.)

3. A collection of prose extracts, chosen on the principles already mentioned.

4. If a complete play, then, for preference, *Henry V*, *A Midsummer Night's Dream*, *Julius Caesar*.

For rapid reading in school or at home, such books as *Kidnapped*, *Ivanhoe*, *Micah Clarke*, *The White Company*, *Tales of a Wayside Inn*.

The age 13–16

Whatever is being read, a background of interest should be secured first, and this may be gained in many different ways according to what is being read, the aptitude of the boys, and the inclination of the teacher. One may dwell on the personality of the writer, the circle in which he lived (*e.g.* Goldsmith)—indeed, this should, in every case, be made clear; another may touch upon the historical setting, or the circumstances which led to the writing of the work, or the prevailing literary ideas of the time (*e.g.* the reason for the heroic couplet of Pope and Dryden, and the different outlook of the Romantic Poets). This introduction should not anticipate the conclusions to be drawn at the end, *e.g.* the fact that Browning was profoundly interested in human nature should be deduced from the reading, not emphasised by way of preparation.

Neither is it well to begin with a short chronological sketch of literature, though it is useful to make a chart in the classroom as the boys become acquainted with various authors.

Further, English teachers in particular should themselves read widely, and in every other possible way keep in touch with the world of culture outside.

1. Syllabus.

As before, reading should include:

(*a*) A good verse anthology, supplemented by the more particular reading of one poet, especially in the years 14–15, 15–16.

(*b*) A play or plays. After the plays which have already been mentioned, *The Merchant of Venice*, *As You Like It*, *Henry IV*, Part I, are suitable. *Macbeth* is a good introduction to the great tragedies, but should not be read before 14. Some boys are ready to read *Hamlet* and even *Lear* by 15, but generally it is better to postpone them till after 16.

Othello is not suitable for school reading, and though selected scenes from *Much Ado About Nothing* are always enjoyed, the play as a whole should not be read before 16. *The Tempest* is read most profitably in the year 15–16, Sheridan's *Rivals* and Goldsmith's Plays in the year 14–15.

(*c*) Prose here should generally take the form of standard Essays, Addison, Steele, Goldsmith, Lamb, Macaulay, Carlyle. It is always interesting and valuable to read Letters side by side with Essays (*e.g.* Lamb's Letters and Essays), just as it is to read North's *Plutarch* side by side with *Julius Caesar*, or Malory with the *Idylls of the King*.

Other prose works suitable for private or rapid reading are Prescott's *Mexico*, Kinglake's *Eöthen*, Selections from Borrow, Stevenson's *Travels in the Cevennes*, many of the *Waverley Novels*, some of Dickens and Thackeray, *The Vicar of Wakefield*, *Pilgrim's Progress*.

There is no reason why good modern plays should not occasionally be read, especially in the year 14–15 (*i.e.* the year before the certificate year). The difficulty of expense stands in the way to some extent, but, given a demand, publishers will generally try to meet it, and it is not necessary for every boy to have a copy. Drinkwater's *Abraham Lincoln* and *Oliver Cromwell*, Galsworthy's *Strife*, Barrie's *Quality Street*, Masefield's *Pompey the Great* are the kind of play suggested. To read them would bring home the fact that plays which are literature are still being written, that there is no divorce between literature and the life of to-day, while it would provide an antidote to the film drama with its insistence on mere incident and its untruthfulness to life. We cannot assign to these plays their exact place in our literature, but we can show that the tradition is still being carried on in new ways, for we should compare the modern outlook with that of the past, and we should try to show that, though much rubbish is being staged to-day, there is work of a very different quality.

Similarly, modern poetry need not be reserved for older boys; the two collections of *Poems of To-day* published by Sidgwick and Jackson for the English Association are very suitable for boys over 13, while a few of Conrad's and Kipling's short stories might sometimes be read to the boys.

2. The Essay.

(*a*) Much reading aloud by the boys is necessary, both to stimulate appreciation and to test it.

(*b*) It is not desirable to break the interest by constant interruptions, but either at the end of the period, or at the beginning of the next, there should be some consideration of what has been read. In a long essay the portion read at any one lesson should, as far as possible, be a complete unit.

(*c*) It is neither necessary nor desirable that the whole of a long essay should be read aloud in class, but some means must be taken to ensure that the silent reading at home or in school is properly done, and that what is read has been appreciated.

(*d*) Where the reading of a long essay has to be spread over a number of lessons, care should be taken at the end to consider it as a whole so that the unity of the theme is not missed.

(*e*) Difficult words and phrases will naturally call for explanation, though it is a moot point whether the precise meaning of every word and phrase need be known, especially by younger boys.

(*f*) Occasional paragraphs and sentences may be considered as examples of construction.

(*g*) The manner in which the writer treats his subject, and his style generally, should not be forgotten, especially with the older boys. Probably the summary when the whole essay, or series of essays, has been read is the best place for this, and the comparative method is extremely valuable (*e.g.* Addison's finished and balanced treatment of the subject compared with Steele's rougher but more spontaneous appeal to our feelings. Which do the boys prefer, and why?).

(*h*) Boys may occasionally learn extracts from short essays, or at least write down striking phrases and memorise them.

(*i*) The question of note-taking is a difficult one. Many successful teachers accustom boys quite early to make their own notes of what is done in class, giving credit for good notes and hardly ever dictating set notes.

(*j*) Occasionally, good modern essays should be read to a class and discussed, especially in comparison with earlier works.

3. The Drama.

(*a*) After consideration, it seems best, in allotting parts, to give the heavier parts to the best readers, so that the general effect is not spoilt, but to take care that no boy is without a part. A good plan is to have understudies to the principal parts and to put them on occasionally, and to give the same boy several minor parts.

(*b*) The first reading should be without a break, and at a fair pace.

(*c*) The structure of the play may then be considered—exposition, entanglement, crisis, etc. Characterisation should next receive attention, varying according to the age of the boys, and amplified during the second reading.

(*d*) The play should then be read a second time, with pauses at intervals to consider what has been read. Some would stop only at the end of a scene, others more frequently, but the pause should never be in the middle of a long speech. Difficulties in wording or construction will be dealt with here, and for this purpose a text with foot-notes is far the best. Wherever the pauses are made, there should be an attempt at the end of each scene to realise its relationship to the rest of the play, and the question of dramatic relief should be touched upon.

(*e*) After the second reading, the play should be considered as a whole and general conclusions drawn. Its source and its relation to other plays will be points for the older boys. A general appreciation of the play can be supplemented by taking select scenes for dramatic rendering, though it is probably more useful for a number of short passages to be learnt by heart than a few long ones, exception being made in favour of those passages which have an intrinsic value apart from their setting in the play. Some latitude in choice will result in greater interest and willingness to learn, and it must always be remembered that some boys learn by heart with much more difficulty than others.

(*f*) In connection with the reading of Shakespeare, some idea of the Elizabethan stage should be given; one member had had a model made in the handicraft class and found it most useful in illustration.

(*g*) Finally, we must not forget that Shakespeare was a poet, and passages must be considered from that point of view. Boys can understand why Titania speaks in poetry, while Bottom speaks in prose, and even realise that Caliban, too, must inevitably speak in poetry.

4. **The Novel.** This form of literature is not suitable for intensive reading in class, and the main object of having such books in the school syllabus should be to show the difference between a good novel and a bad one.

The way in which it can be handled will best be shown by taking an example such as *Treasure Island*.

(*a*) As introduction, a description of actual pirates could be given, together with the way in which the conditions in the Spanish Main during the eighteenth century led to piracy. As a boy, Stevenson was fascinated by pirate tales, so that he came in later life to write this romance for other boys.

(*b*) Private reading by the boys follows.

(*c*) After reading, an examination of the plot and construction. Are the incidents probable or possible? Do they lead naturally from one to another?

(*d*) Far more important is the question of the characters. Do they behave and do they talk as such people would be expected to behave? Are the characters and the incidents in which they figure consistent? In a word, are they real?

(*e*) All these points can be emphasised by the intensive reading of occasional chapters, and by comparison with the blood and thunder story read by boys, where one can point out the impossibility of the incidents, their want of consistency, the absurdity of the dialogue, and the essential unreality of the characters. The perfect naturalness of the way in which Jim Hawkins overheard the plotting when he was in the apple-barrel could be set side by side with some far-fetched, improbable coincidence used in the other type of book.

In dealing with historical novels, it should be shown that strict adherence to historical fact is not necessary if the spirit of history is kept and the historical background is true, and if the picture of the social life of the time is accurate. Always, truth in the depiction of character should be kept in the foreground, and the fact made clear that the great writer does not need to tell us what people are like, but shows us this in their conversations and actions.

A few boys can be brought to enjoy the description of natural scenery in such books as *Westward Ho!*, *Lorna Doone*, *Jane Eyre*, especially if they know something of the country described.

The Novel of Manners such as *Pride and Prejudice* is not generally suitable for school reading under the age of 16. A book like *Pickwick Papers* is, for one can show that in spite of exaggeration, faults of style and of construction, the characters are real and the book abounding in vitality.

Needless to say, the wise teacher will not try to arrive at such results by telling the class those facts, but will by conversation and questions lead the boys to suggest them, so training their critical faculties that they will be able to judge other novels for themselves.

Apart from novels dealt with in the way suggested, there should be plenty of others available in form libraries or school libraries. It is often found that, when a novel by an author is successfully handled in school, there is a demand for others by the same writer.

Room should be found for a few novels of the best modern writers. Wells (at any rate his scientific romances and sociological studies), Winston Churchill (*Coniston*, *Richard Carvel*), some of De Morgan's, Hardy's *Under the Greenwood Tree*, are tentative suggestions. Collections of short stories by Kipling, Edgar Allan Poe, Conan Doyle, Bret Harte, are best left to the library, though an occasional reading by the master will direct attention to them.

Finally, the deep and varied knowledge essential to the writing of a good novel—so often the record of personal experience—should not be overlooked.

5. **The Ballad.** After the introductory talk the ballad should be read through once quickly, generally by the master. Then a second time, more slowly, to clear up difficulties as they are encountered. At the end, a general talk, when it should be made clear that the effect is often irrespective of the truth or otherwise of the incidents. The question of form and metre is better postponed till a number of ballads have been read. Then it is valuable to set as an exercise the writing of a short ballad, or a few quatrains on some suitable modern subject, *e.g.* "The Voyage of the Quest."

The main points to notice about the ballad are the striking impression left on the imagination by the poems as a whole, the strong dramatic note, the way in which the story revolves round a hero or heroine, the frequent sense of mystery, and the metre. Older boys will see how a cycle of ballads evolves into an epic.

Owing to the unevenness, few of the older ballads should be learnt by heart, and, with them all, it should be realised how the whole poem is greater than any part.

The Ancient Mariner stands by itself for special treatment, but it may be discussed in comparison with the older ballads.

6. **Lyrical Poetry.** Some lyrical poetry should be read at all stages in a boy's career. The master should almost always read the poem first aloud to the class, so that the effect may not be spoiled. Indeed, the personality of the teacher shows itself nowhere so markedly as in dealing with lyrical poetry.

A striking instance was given of the method by which boys could be taught a new lyric by the way in which it was read and re-read to the class. If this is not possible for the majority, yet that is how the spirit of the lyric will be impressed upon the boys.

To formulate methods of treating the lyric is not easy, for some which have proved most successful with some teachers will prove lifeless and mechanical in the hands of others. One, for instance, will write on the blackboard a string of words suggesting the thoughts which passed through the poet's mind, and gradually group round these the words of the poem. It is argued that thus will the class appreciate and understand the feeling which lies behind the words, and the skill with which the poet has expressed that feeling.

A number follow Mr Greening Lambourn in holding that

the way of approach is through music; that music and lyrical poetry are two closely related modes of expressing the same emotions.

All meet on common ground in believing that the main point to be made clear is that the lyric is the expression of deep and sincere feeling in harmonious sounds. First we must begin by showing what the feelings were that the poet experienced; that those feelings were deep and strong and very real; indeed, that a man can only be a lyrical poet if he has a faculty for such feelings. There must never be a suspicion that the poet looks round for a subject, and, after selecting one, weaves a web of smooth verses round it as a sort of exercise in handling words. Then we try to show the beauty of sound, and how the poet uses sound to convey to us the feeling within him. Prose would be quite inadequate, just as a pen or pencil will not satisfy a great painter setting out to convey to us what he sees in a landscape. Again, the poet sings because he must, just as a child must dance when a barrel organ plays a jig-tune.

The choice of words can be explained—why in one place "steed" is the only possible word, where in another it must be "horse." The subtle distinction between "fairy" and "faery" is not beyond the comprehension of many boys.

The close connection between the prosody of a poem and its subject is important. Just as a boy learning music must understand changes of time, so one reading poetry should appreciate changes of metre. Why, in *Christabel*, the measure quickens as the interest is raised, why *Il Penseroso* has a different metrical character from *L'Allegro*, are examples of what is meant.

Always, however, the aim we should have in mind is the ability to distinguish between the good and the bad, not merely in a general and vague way, but with real understanding.

7. **Experiment and Experience.** At no other stage of the investigations has the Committee found evidence of a greater amount of experiment and a greater variety of experience than at this. As an indication there are set out below a number of individual opinions and suggestions, sometimes in the form of notes. They are to be read as illustrations of what is being done, and not necessarily as recommendations by the Committee.

A. Music and Literature—A Suggestion

"Poetry is music. The melody lies in the words and in the poet's harmonious arrangement of them. The choice of words and the arrangement of them are, then, matters for the poet himself, and so, with poets as with musicians, we get different melodies and harmonies, *e.g.*,

A {
1. Nash's 'Song of Spring'—*Spring, the sweet Spring, is the Year's pleasant King.*
2. Shakespeare's 'The —*It was a lover and his lass.* Spring of Love'
}

B {
3. Mendelssohn's 'Spring Song.'
4. Sinding's 'Rustle of Spring.'
}

The interpretation of (1) and of (2) is as different as the interpretation of (3) and of (4), but there is melody and harmony in each of them.

There is some parallel, then, between A and B; both have measured and harmonious sound. The difference lies in the expression of the melody; our voices are the only instruments for A.

The metre might be compared with the tune of a song. Cf. various chords and discords in Music with various sounds in Poetry.

Selections of good music could be played to show the effects of different measures and for comparison with different rhythms in Poetry, *e.g.*,

1. *Martial*   (*a*) Marche des Troubadours.
             (*b*) Marche aux Flambeaux.

2. *Tripping*   (*a*) Mendelssohn's 'Spring Song.'
             (*b*) Dvorak's 'Humoreske.'

3. *Stately*   Handel's 'Largo.'

4. *Mournful* (*a*) 'Dead March in Saul.'
             (*b*) Ase's Death—'Peer Gynt' (Grieg).
             (*c*) Chopin—Prelude No. 20.

Attention should be called to the suitability of different forms to express different kinds of thoughts.

Words of songs should possess real literary merit. A body of good poetry could be built up in this way alone, and certainly only good could come from the constant association of good poetry with good music. There are plenty of old Folk Songs and lyrics of Shakespeare and poets down to the present day to choose from.

Exercises. These would help the boys to appreciate the appropriateness of the various forms.

(*a*) Choose a simple air and select some lyric to fit it.

(*b*) Choose a simple air and make an original verse or poem to fit it.

(*c*) Write an original verse or poem and fit it to an air.

(*d*) Write down an original verse or poem and try to compose an original air for it.

Now a little discussion beforehand would soon bring out that it would not do to write a poem like *Annie Laurie, Robin Adair* or *Drink to Me Only* and fit it to the tune of *The British Grenadiers, John Peel*, or the *Men of Harlech*, and *vice versa*.

The measure must be in harmony with the spirit of the content.

In Note F to his *Poetry for Poetry's Sake*, Dr Bradley writes: ' I see no reason why an exceedingly competent person should not try to indicate the emotional tone of a composition, movement, or passage, or the changes of feeling within it, or even, very roughly, the "idea" he may suppose it to embody (though he need not imply that the composer had any of this before his mind). And I believe that such indications, however inadequate they must be, may greatly help the uneducated lover of music to hear more truly the music itself.'

I do not think that only an '*exceedingly* competent' person is capable of doing this—most of us could do it in some degree. But even so the Music Master should be called in to help. A better understanding between Music Masters and English Masters would lead to a keener appreciation of English Literature and Music."

B. Poetry that Boys Like

" In poetry every boy's taste differs from his neighbour's. What is disliked is

(*a*) The sentimental, *e.g.*, *The May Queen*.

(*b*) The Sunday-school lyric, *e.g.*, *We are Seven*.

(*c*) The vociferous type, *e.g.*, much of Byron's work; what of Byron *is* liked, is liked very much.

(*d*) The heavy: many of Wordsworth's moralising poems.

As for what is liked, perhaps a partial list may be useful:

Imaginative poems, *e.g.*,

> *The Ancient Mariner*.
> *The Highland Reaper*.

Poems which give pleasurable mental pictures, *e.g.*,

> *The Palace of Art.*
> *The Lady of Shalott.*

Poems vigorous in metre or outlook, *e.g.*,

> Masefield's work.
> *Childe Roland to the Dark Tower came*; and much else of Browning.

Narrative poems where the story seems worth telling, *e.g.*,

> *Idylls of the King.*
> *Sohrab and Rustum.*

Poems pleasing to the ear, or where skill in sound-manipulation is shown, *e.g.*,

> Some of Robert Bridges' work.
> Swinburne.

Unclassified 'popular' poets and poems:

> Rupert Brooke.
> Wordsworth's nature poetry, where he does not moralise too much.
> Very much of Tennyson.
> Milton. (Appeals to the elect; though he inspires awe rather than love.)
> Keats' Odes; and (in one or two cases) *Endymion*.
> As an anthology, *Poems of To-day* (and the new set) appeals strongly to the older boys.
> William Watson, *Wordsworth's Grave*.

I have not tried Vachel Lindsay yet; I fancy he would be distinctly popular.

Shelley does not seem to take the fancy. 'Too vague and misty.'

The 18th century is too earth-bound to attract, and boys *never* voluntarily choose the heroic couplet when writing original verse.

Stuart poets are too metaphysical, in general.

Vers libre makes no appeal at all."

C. Three Typical Lists of Books Read

"(*a*) Age 13–14.

Tales from Shakespeare (Lamb)	
Ulysses (Lamb)	
Morte D'Arthur	Detailed
An anthology (*Coronata*)—selections from	study.
Hiawatha	
The Lay of the Last Minstrel	

Gulliver's Travels
Treasure Island
Travels with a Donkey } Rapid reading.
Treasure Trove

Age 14–15.

English Humorists
Boswell's *Johnson*—selection
Spectator Papers—selection
Macbeth } In detail.
Henry V
A Midsummer Night's Dream
The Rivals

Anthology (*Coronata* or Edgar's Part IV)
Poems of To-day } Rapid
Kenilworth reading.
A Tale of Two Cities, etc.

Age 15–16.

Works prescribed for General School Exam. (London University).

(b) Age 12–13.

Hiawatha
The Lady of the Lake
Macaulay's *Lays* } Detailed study.
Carmina Britanniae (selected poems)
Lee: *Selections from English Lit.* Book I

Beowulf
Ivanhoe } Etc., well represented in Form
The Talisman Libraries for rapid reading.
In Golden Realms

Age 13–14.

Henry IV, Part I
Henry V } Detailed study.
A Midsummer Night's Dream
Lee: *Selections from English Lit.* Book I

Quentin Durward
In the World of Books
Pilgrim's Progress } Etc., in Form Libraries
Gulliver's Travels for rapid reading.
Westward Ho!
The Cloister and the Hearth

Age 14–15.

> Chaucer: *Prologue*
>   *Nun Priest's Tale*
>   *Prioress's Tales*
> *Julius Caesar*
> *Twelfth Night*   Detailed study.
> *The Faery Queene*, I or V
> *Spectator* Papers
> *Golden Treasury* (in part, especially
>   *L'Allegro* and *Il Penseroso*)

> *Kenilworth*   } Etc., in Form Libraries for
> *A Tale of Two Cities* }   rapid reading.

(c) Age 11–13.

> *Water Babies.*
> *Robinson Crusoe.*
> *Peter Pan* (Barrie's prose version).
> *Gulliver's Travels* (Parts I and II).
> *Treasure Island.*
> Smith's *Book of Verse.*
> *Child's Garden of Verses.*
> *Hiawatha.*
> *The Ancient Mariner.*
> *John Gilpin.*

Age 13–14.

> *Malory* (simplified version).
> *The Vicar of Wakefield.*
> Lamb's *Adventures of Ulysses.*
> *The Deserted Village.*
> *A Book of Ballads.*
> *Sohrab and Rustum.*

> *Hereward the Wake* }
> *Lorna Doone*   } Rapid reading.

Age 14–15.

> *Rip Van Winkle*, etc.
> *Cranford.*
> *Bible Anthology.*
> *The Golden Treasury.*
> *Macbeth.*
> Tennyson (Selections).

> *David Copperfield* }
> *Legend of Montrose* } Rapid reading.
> *Silas Marner*   }

Age 15–16.

> *The Coverley Papers.*
> *Selected English Essays.*
> *The Rivals.*
> Chaucer's *Prologue.*
> *Henry V.*
>
> *Vanity Fair*
> *The Cloister and the Hearth* } Rapid reading."
> *Pride and Prejudice*

D. Methods of Study

"*The Lore of the Wanderer*: an Anthology of the Open Air (prose). The King's Treasuries.

(1) Nature Writing in English Literature—appreciation of Nature (general).
  Cf. word pictures in poetry—recall poems known.
  Here *essay* form.

  Discuss points such as (*a*) desire to wander; (*b*) pre-possessions in mind of wanderer—which colour his observations; (*c*) objects of observation: birds, flowers, scenery, etc.; (*d*) life of a recluse; (*e*) vivid pen pictures; (*f*) wanderings abroad.

(2) Note *literary expression* of such experiences.

(3) *Study of the Essay* (*e.g.*, with Macaulay).

  (*a*) Subject-matter—all kinds of subjects—other essayists—(books can be read in Library).

  (*b*) Treatment as varied as subject-matter itself. Note in this anthology—unity of subject-matter but great variety of treatment, leads to discussion of *style.*

  (*c*) Knowledge of author—from the essays. This forms an introduction to a talk on *Personality in Literature* (without using this phrase). Knowledge of facts in author's life as help in appreciating his work, *e.g.*, Stevenson and his wanderings.

  (*d*) *Structure of the Essay:*

  (i) Varieties of beginning.

  (ii) Middle—arrangement of matter—study of paragraphs. Cf. Macaulay.

  (iii) Variety of conclusion.

Exercises in analysing structure.

(e) *Choice of words*—right word in right place.
Substitute synonyms for words and phrases and examine effect.

(f) *Figures of Speech*—how they help expression and give beauty.

(g) *Allusions and quotations*—their fitness.

(h) *Rhythm in prose.* If the ear has been trained, reading aloud is a test of appreciation by boys. Appreciation can be tested by degree of interest aroused in boys—by mode of reading, discussions, written questions, *e.g.*, preference for particular essays, characters, etc.

Most of these points would be taken after the boys had read particular essays by themselves. Time will not allow of all the essays being read in class."

E. The Merchant of Venice

"(1) Rapid reading at home.

(2) Analysis of structure—Acts and Scenes.

(3) How each scene contributes to the development of the plot and action.

(4) The personages: (a) chief characters; (b) minor characters; (c) development of character; *e.g.*, effect of certain events on Bassanio and Portia. First, preliminary study of chief personages—to be followed by a closer study of their development; then of the minor characters—purpose of introducing these—their degree of importance.

(5) The plot; several stories go to make the plot; how these stories are mingled should be shown.

(6) Class reading of certain scenes. Appreciation helped and tested by manner of acting in interpreting characters."

F. Methods of Cultivating Appreciation and of Testing it

"Treat the work as a practical natural product pulsating with life. Acting will help with the drama. Home Reading must be referred to often and encouraged; and if a notebook can be kept by each boy it will be a great stimulus to the intelligent boys. Lyrics should be related to the whole work of the poet and shown not to be spasmodic whimsies; the isolation of lyrics often leads to false ideas on the whole subject of poetry; a man behind the poem is a new idea to many boys. Parody may help sometimes; or a prose expansion. If the class is sympathetic and the teacher well read in psychology, much may be gained by suggestive explanations on psychological grounds, *e.g.*, why men should produce lyric poems at all. The class criticism will give both training and evidence of progress. Then a debating society will assist; form libraries; school plays; papers by the cleverer boys; and many others.

Optional verse-writing; play-acting; all plays to be roughly acted on the first reading, and later certain scenes to be learnt and performed more carefully.

A form notebook to be kept for entering good original work done during the year; a form magazine encouraged.

Comparisons drawn between different writers in a simple way; and after each piece of work read a short criticism; after selected ones, a blackboard criticism by the form to be made, with illustrations and conclusions, thus:

Story or Argument: In brief outline.

Suitability: Yes or no, and reason. Too many plots? Work out well? Convincing?

Characters: Three chief outlined; convincing or not; humorous or not. Could you meet them at any moment in the street?

Style: Hard or easy? Quick or slow? Beautiful or not? Examples, if verse, of alliteration, onomatopœia, and other devices.

General Conclusion: Sum up the class impression.

Of course, it would not have to be done mechanically, as this seems to suggest; but each work would suggest its own treatment to the teacher. It is a class talk on the book and a final dismissal of it. Growth in taste will be revealed by the criticisms offered."

G. Home Reading and the way to encourage it

"Judicious questioning shows that despite interest of parts, much of these books are not really interesting to boys of these ages. It is even at best a forced interest. And this is natural, for experience of life is not deep enough or wide enough to catch on to the numerous points hidden in the books. They were written by adults for adult minds, and it is no compliment to authors to expect very young minds really to like them.

Throw overboard the idea of a 'class' during appreciation lessons. Treat the 'period' as a chance for free discussion, and encourage boys to talk freely. Talk with and to them—do not lecture. Let the boys indicate the beauties of what is read. Their taste is sometimes sounder than ours,—though not always.

Treat the class as fellow-explorers and set them hunting for examples of literary artifice, *e.g.*, alliterations, 'comparisons' (simile and metaphor), apt epithets, fine bits of description, fine ideas, etc.; encourage emulation in making and reporting such discoveries and in keeping a scrap-book for entry of chosen phrases and extracts, statement of reasons for choice being encouraged."

H. Composition through Story Writing

"Among the experiments in teaching composition through story writing, perhaps the most ambitious is the most interesting. The class was encouraged to attempt the writing of a complete treasure island story based upon the life of William Phips, who discovered treasure in the 17th century and became the first Governor of Massachusetts. His life as set out in *The Book of Buried Treasure* by Ralph D. Payne formed the basis of the plot, though any members of the class were allowed to depart from this if reasons were sufficient.

For half a term the class worked an intensive course of composition disguised by the name, 'The Craft of the Author'— exercises in narration, description, characterisation, plot construction, etc., and only when a member had proved himself story-worth could he begin his own romance. Throughout the two terms during which the story was being written, lessons were given supplementary to this introductory course. Paragraphs and chapters from master mariners who had sailed these seas of romance were studied in an endeavour to learn the 'rule of the road' that had brought them to success. Books which had once interested for the story alone were re-read in order to discover the manner of the telling of the story. The children began to see the author at work, facing the very obstacles that hindered their own progress and overcoming them in a way which they now, for the first time, began to appreciate. They realised the important truth that the story of *Treasure Island* is the story of a hundred-and-one third rate treasure island stories, but that it differs from them in the care and sincerity with which it is written.

Some admittedly tired of the story. They were set to work to compile dossiers of information on the climate of the island, the history of shipping at that period, the flora and fauna of our island, etc. A mutiny on the lower desks was settled by a course in verse composition, when our mutineers became the jolly shanty men of the party. Some idea of the enthusiasm aroused can be appreciated by the fact that some stories ran to between twenty and thirty thousand words."

I. Libraries

" Each Form should have its own library, and this library should contain as great variety of books as possible.

In a Form of 25 boys a library was started in the following way. Each boy was asked to bring a book and *give* it to the library. He soon saw that for his one book he would be able to read 24 others. Some boys brought two books, some six—they bring books for the library when they like. Parents became interested and helped. One Form has got together more than 200 books in less than a year.

It will be found, however, that where the formation of the library depends on the generosity of the boys the majority of the books will be fiction, which means that the position of the *School* Library as the home of Classics and books of reference at once commands a greater respect and assumes a rôle of greater importance by virtue of comparison with its lesser lights in the Form rooms.

The Form Library, then, would provide a large number of good books for recreative reading—books which would be denied to *individuals* owing to their cost.

The libraries, which actually belong to the boys and are always available, have proved a great incentive to reading. But the teacher's part must be a very active one. He must try to appreciate the tastes of each boy and be careful not to condemn a book without giving reasons for doing so. Indeed, he should very rarely condemn; failure to give any reasons at all would certainly have a most undesirable effect.

You cannot prevent a boy from reading what he will, but you can show him the merits and demerits of any book and lead him quietly and sympathetically on to something better.

Ask him what he thinks about the book he is reading—encourage him to come to you at any time to discuss it with you. Ask him whether he likes it better than the last one he read and why. Lead him on to compare the plots and the characters—you are then setting him out on the road of criticism.

Encouragement, not indifference, must be the guiding principle of the teacher. He should make every possible use of the Form Libraries; it will increase their importance, stimulate interest, and show what pleasure can be got from the inside of books. The boys will see that the value of the book does not rest on the cover."

CHAPTER V

ENGLISH IN EXAMINATIONS

The First School Examination

The work in English during the year 15–16, in state-aided secondary schools and in many others also, is almost entirely determined by the requirements of the First School Examinations which the boys will be taking at the end of the year.

The harm that follows this limitation of the aims and scope of the teaching is most regrettable, particularly because in the great majority of cases this year is the last in a boy's school life; but it is unavoidable. The following quotations from the Report of the School Examinations Council, taken from the Report of the Board of Education for the School Year, 1924–25, lay down the lines upon which reforms should proceed, *and are especially applicable to First School Examinations in English:*

"The main purpose of the First School Examinations being to provide an adequate test of the work of the average candidate from the average school at about the age of 16, it follows that the papers should be easy in character. It will then be fair to mark them strictly and to exact a high mark for credit."

"The desire to set questions which are 'interesting' or which may be expected to guide and perhaps to improve the work of the schools is no doubt a natural one, but such questions may not be consistent with the main purpose of the examination and if they are too hard for the average candidate may, in fact, defeat it. There is a danger in stimulating and guiding school work by means of an external examination—*the danger that the teaching may follow the lines of the examination instead of, as far as possible, the examination those of the teaching.*"

"Easy papers can be marked expeditiously and strictly, and they separate candidates much more effectively and much more fairly than papers which are even only a little too difficult and the marking of which is, therefore, necessarily more lenient."

The Revising Committee is in full agreement with the dicta of the School Examinations Council. It follows that both syllabuses and papers should be framed to suit the requirements not so much of the small minority of candidates who will proceed to Universities as for the great majority who will not take up academic careers. Examiners too often have that minority in their minds when setting papers, and yield to the temptation "to guide the work of the schools."

Nor should questions only be "easy in character"; they should be worded in simple, direct English, and in particular they should be entirely free from the least suspicion of ambiguity. Questions on set books should deal with main features, not with unusual or exceptional points; they should assume no more than the bare minimum of information, apart from the subject-matter, required for a proper understanding and appreciation of the books themselves.

The following notes refer, in the main, to the form which papers in English should take:

1. There should be a liberal choice of subjects for essay, appealing to many different tastes and capabilities. They should include historical, geographical, literary, descriptive, narrative and argumentative subjects, all within the range of the pupils' experience, knowledge, or imagination. The object should be to test not specialised knowledge but the power to write good connected English. The essay should form a separate paper and should have sufficient time allotted to it.

2. There should be a précis of a continuous passage, a dialogue, or a short correspondence between two or three people. The original should have literary value.

3. Other suitable exercises in writing are letters, dialogues and the answering of advertisements.

4. Grammar questions should be optional and should be concerned with essential points and not with obscure details of syntax—it is doubtful whether historic survivals or archaic forms should be set in this examination.

5. Questions testing the correct use of words may be included.

6. General questions on prosody and the figures of speech.

7. Questions on style should be optional, *not* compulsory, and the extracts given should be long enough for the candidate to show some real appreciation; they should not be a line or two to test the recognition of some figure of speech or some trick of poetic diction. Some would confine these questions on style to the set books read, and even then would make them quite general, *e.g.* What is the charm of Lamb? The danger in

both cases is that the candidate may merely repeat opinions expressed by the teacher and embodied in some note. Examiners might make more use of the type of question where the candidate is asked to illustrate some characteristic of the writer by references to what he has read, either generally or with the help of quotations.

A few welcome a question where two long quotations on similar subjects are given for comparison (*e.g.* Cowper's *Lines on his Mother's Portrait* and Eliza Cook's *The Old Armchair*). They think that it does provide a real test of appreciation for the better candidates; others think such a question too advanced—over the heads of boys of sixteen.

8. There is universal approval of the setting of books to be read, but there should be a considerable choice allowed to the teacher, and a distinction made between books studied intensively and those read in a general way. The books should represent no form of specialised study, whether of a period or of a school of literature, but the general measure of culture expected to be reached by boys of sixteen. A play of Shakespeare, a writer of the seventeenth century, one of the eighteenth, and a modern, for instance, with a fair division between prose and poetry, are suggested as a suitable syllabus.

The questions set should not be of the kind that might be answered without reading a word of the text but by cramming up some handbook, nor should they be concerned with some minute and obscure detail. At least one question on a set book should deal mainly with subject-matter and require no more than a competent understanding of it. There is a strong feeling about the type of context question where the passage given is short, of no distinctive meaning, and without any particular bearing on the larger passage in which it occurs; indeed, many would cut out the context questions altogether because they tend to become pointless and therefore are no test of appreciation.

Questions where candidates are asked for lists of books and authors are valueless.

An interesting suggestion for the choice of set books is given, which would save a master from having to read again some book dealt with at an earlier age, unless he preferred it.

1. General Reading $\begin{cases} (a) \text{ Prose Books. } 3 \text{ books.} \\ (b) \text{ Verse.} \qquad\qquad ,, \end{cases}$

2. Special Study $\left\{\begin{array}{ll}(c) & \text{Drama.} \qquad \text{3 books.} \\ (d) & \text{Prose.} \qquad\qquad \text{,,} \\ (e) & \text{Verse.} \qquad\qquad \text{,,}\end{array}\right.$

One to be chosen from each section (a), (b), (c), (d), (e).

The following are two individual opinions with which, however, the Revising Committee is in full agreement:

(i) "Contexts are made harder by being mixed at haphazard in one question embracing all the books set for special reading. They sometimes appear to have been chosen deliberately to trip up candidates, *e.g.* a passage from *The Pilgrim's Progress* mentioning Rome in the same question as 'context' passages from *Coriolanus*. The questions on Shakespeare are sometimes too difficult. In one year *Coriolanus* was set for both School Certificate and Higher School Certificate (Full and Subsidiary). In the former paper a question on the play ran something like the following: '"Coriolanus's banishment from Rome was due less to political jobbery than to faults in his own character." Discuss this.' In the H.S.C. (Subsidiary) paper merely a straightforward character sketch—of Menenius, I think—was demanded. Both in Shakespeare 'contexts' and questions on appreciation the examiners appear to try to avoid the obvious questions. Is this quite fair, or likely to produce the most useful teaching?"

. (ii) "The context question should be on fairly long passages and those both significant and excellently written."

A MODEL FIRST SCHOOL EXAMINATION
(*An Individual Opinion*)

The papers should consist of:

Essay. At least a dozen subjects. They should never overlap, should be absolutely free from ambiguity, and should include at least six titles likely to appeal to the non-literary boy.

Précis. There should be a choice between two or three pieces: narrative, descriptive, prose, poetry, letters, passages from law court proceedings, or from evidence before Committees and Commissions, dialogue. They should *never* be reflective, abstract or philosophical.

Essay, Précis. One paper. *Time:* 2 hours.

Marks: Essay, 20 %; Précis, 15 % of total.

General English. The questions should include *none* but the following types:

(a) sentences for comment and correction;

(b) an unpunctuated passage, possibly partly in direct and partly in indirect speech, to be re-written correctly;

(c) a passage in clumsy, possibly verbose and involved but not necessarily ungrammatical English, to be re-written but not condensed;

(d) a passage in which various figures of speech are to be identified and explained (much literature, *e.g.* the Bible, is misread because it is figurative);

(e) the analysis of sentences into clauses and the stating of their inter-relationships. The "functions," not the full parsing, of phrases and words, may fairly be asked;

(f) synthesis;

(g) the writing of a letter or a paragraph from a given word-outline;

(h) poetry for scansion;

(i) synonyms and antonyms;

(j) the detection of simple fallacies (no technical terms to be required).

Time: $1\frac{1}{2}$ hours (3 questions).

Marks: 20 % of total.

Literature. Syllabus:

Special. A. Candidates to present *one* book from each of the following lists:

(a) Shakespeare: 10 plays given;

(b) the Classics: 10–20 books given.

General. B. Candidates to present *three* books, *one* from *each* of the following lists:

(a) six modern essays and miscellanea;

(b) six modern novels;

(c) six modern plays.

Questions on *A* (intensive reading) to be of present-day type, but simple and direct.

Questions on *B* (general reading) to be so framed as to do no more than test first-hand knowledge and understanding of subject-matter.

A choice between at least three questions from each book.

No questions on style or literary qualities of *B* books.

Books not Set. C.

Five questions on recent literature, not included in above syllabus, so designed as to test first-hand knowledge and understanding only of books on which questions are asked.

One question to be answered from each of the subsections *A* (*a*), *A* (*b*), *B* (*a*), *B* (*b*) and *B* (*c*), but a candidate to be allowed to answer a question from *C* in lieu of one from the subsections *B* (*a*), *B* (*b*), *B* (*c*).

Time: $2\frac{1}{2}$ hours. *Marks:* 45 % of total.

"Recent" defined as written after, say, 1880.

Recent or Present-Day Literature Suitable for First School Examination

At the suggestion of the Education Committee of the Association, the Revising Committee invited corresponding members to send lists of "set books," suitable for First School Examinations, in recent English Literature (*i.e.* written during the past 50 years or so). The following lists have been compiled from their replies. Obviously, some of the books recommended are suitable for intensive study, others for general reading.

ESSAYS

Stevenson: *Virginibus Puerisque; Familiar Studies of Men and Books.*
Quiller-Couch: *Dickens and Other Victorians.*
Masefield: *Gallipoli.*
Belloc: *On Nothing, and Kindred Subjects; Hills and the Sea.*
Birrell: *Obiter Dicta.*
Robert Lynd: *Selected Essays.*
Gardiner: *Alpha of the Plough.*

Also:
Modern Essays from "The Times." (Arnold.)
Modern Essays. (King's Treasuries.)
Lore of the Wanderer. (King's Treasuries.)
Modern Essays. (Ed. Pritchard.)
Junior Modern Essays. (Dent.)
Essays of To-day. (Harrap.)
Essays by Modern Masters. (Methuen.)

DRAMA

Drinkwater: *Abraham Lincoln; Oliver Cromwell.*
Shaw: *John Bull's Other Island; Arms and the Man; St Joan.*
Barrie: *Quality Street; The Will;* and others.
Galsworthy: *Loyalties; Strife; Justice.*
Housman, L.: *Little Plays of St Francis;* and others.
Chesterton: *The Defendant.*
Arnold Bennett: *Milestones; The Great Adventure.*

Also:
Nine Modern Plays. (Nelson.)
Marriott's *One Act Plays.* (First Series only.) (Harrap.)

NOVELS

Conrad: *Typhoon; Lord Jim; Youth* and *Gaspar Ruiz; Four Stories.* (Dent.)
Arnold Bennett: *Clayhanger.*

Kipling: *Kim.*
Wells: *Food of the Gods; War of the Worlds; First Men in the Moon.*
Hardy: *Under the Greenwood Tree.*
Weyman: *Under the Red Robe; Chippinge;* and others.
Conan Doyle: *The White Company; Micah Clarke.*
M. Hewlett: *The Queen's Quhair;* several others.
Walpole: *Jeremy; Jeremy and Hamlet.*
Mason: *The Four Feathers.*
Vachell: *The Hill;* and, possibly, its sequel.

OTHER TYPES

Chesterton: *St Francis of Assisi.*
A. Saintsbury: *A Letter Book.*

Second School Examination: Higher Certificate

The Committee does not propose to set out in detail syllabuses of advanced work in English, but rather to outline the aims with which the work should be planned and the methods which have been found well adapted to realise these aims.

The great aim, whether English is a main subject or only a subsidiary one, should be the cultivation of literary taste, especially in the direction of widening and developing the pupils' interests. This is true of all the English work done in secondary schools, but should be specially so of the last years of the school course. "It is upon the success of the post-matriculation years that the choice of later reading largely depends, and this is of supreme importance if education is a preparation for life, as in a wide and general sense it should be."

If this is to be the chief aim, it follows that the English master alone should not be responsible for training a boy's powers of expression. The framing of arguments, the marshalling of facts, and the clear expression of ideas should also be the concern of those teaching other subjects in the course. At present much valuable time is taken up in the English hours in attention to these points, and this time can be ill spared from the reading and discussion of literature. The English master should have a share, probably a large share, but still only a share, in this side of the work.

On the other hand, in many advanced courses English is the subject which must provide to a large extent the cultural element, so that it is doubly necessary that the course should be planned on broad lines; opportunities should be sought for provoking intellectual interests of various kinds. Probably in class there is not much time to spare, but occasional discussions will help, while the promotion of literary, dramatic, and debating societies, and of magazine clubs will be part of the English master's activities. In this connection it is most important that some scope should be given to the creative instinct by the encouragement of original writing. It is a general opinion that young children often produce interesting and talented work, but that in the middle part of the school career this is rare, while, at the stage we are considering, the desire and the taste for such writing is again strong. We should do all we can to foster this. Some form of magazine, apart from the official school magazine, is perhaps as good an outlet as possible for such efforts; discreet encouragement and no rigid censorship are to be commended.

The next consideration is that some of these boys may go on to the University, and all, we hope, will continue in some form or other the reading begun at school. It is therefore very important that they should be accustomed to read for themselves, to make notes, to consult books of reference, and sometimes to make up their minds between conflicting opinions. Whatever may be thought of the Dalton plan in general, it is clear that some method of assigning definite work to be done by the pupils themselves under the general guidance and assistance of the teacher must be followed. Any questions of scholarship (*e.g.* the origin and dates of Shakespeare plays read), which have been deferred, can now be handled profitably.

Along what lines should the work proceed to realise these aims and give scope to these methods? There is no simple answer. Many find the solution by tracing the historical development of English literature, so that in a two years' course the outstanding writers from Chaucer to the present day have received some attention. It is agreed that there must be this wide range of reading, and that the choice of books read should be based upon some definite principle, and it is probable that no other scheme will ensure the realisation of these aims.

A typical two years' syllabus suggested by a correspondent on these lines is the following:

1st Year.
    Term 1. Chaucer, Spenser, Malory.
       ,,   2. Elizabethan Drama, Bacon.
       ,,   3. Milton, Herrick, Browne's *Religio Medici.*

2nd Year.
    Term 1. Dryden or Pope, Addison, Burke, Boswell.
       ,,   2. Wordsworth, Coleridge, Keats, Shelley (most in selections, one poet more fully), Lamb, Hazlitt.
  * ,,   3. Tennyson, Browning, Carlyle or Ruskin.

In this type of syllabus the general survey will in itself be sufficient, and there will hardly be time or opportunity for more intensive study apart from it. Some think it so valuable to study a particular period more intensively that they reduce the scope of the general survey—not in width, but in depth— and side by side take some chosen period of English literature. There is no objection to this, provided that the general survey does not become the merest tasting at many tables, or worse still, the remembering of names with little or no knowledge of the books themselves. Similarly, the special period of English literature may well coincide with the period of history studied, but it is not right that the literature to be read should be decided solely by the fact that a particular period of history is prescribed in some examination. It does not seem advisable to concentrate attention on the development of some form of literature, or of some attitude towards literature, *e.g.* the novel, or the romantic movement, for this is calculated to defeat the aim of a wide range and of appealing to many diverse tastes. True, there will be variety, both of authors and of treatment, but this is not all; lyric poetry may appeal to one who is left cold by the reading of many plays.

Some authorities have argued against the wide range of reading, preferring that the pupils should concentrate on the works of a few authors. They maintain that in this way alone can the maximum benefit be derived from the time allotted to English in an Advanced Course, where Examination requirements can be ignored. For the reasons stated above, the Committee is strongly of the opinion that whatever value this

---

* Where an examination has to be taken in the last term, the work may have to be slightly re-arranged.

method may have for the exceptional boy it is a mistaken method when we are dealing with a class of boys varying in capacity and taste.

Since the formation of a critical taste is one of the aims of advanced work, the reading of some critical work on the original author should be encouraged. For example, after reading and discussing *Macbeth*, some boys were introduced to A. C. Bradley on Shakespearean Tragedy. By doing so they probably came to a truer realisation of what tragedy really means than if they had read the play, discussed it, and passed on. There should be in every school a reference library, where such books are to be found. There is a bitter complaint that where libraries exist they are starved of books, and many teachers would like to see the Board of Education ear-mark part of the special grant for the purchase of books.

The reference library should be planned so that, in addition to texts, there should be a place for such modern books as Wyld's *Growth of English*, Ker's *Epic and Romance*, Walker's *Victorian Literature*, Saintsbury's *Loci Critici*, Schelling's *English Drama*, Rhys's *Lyric Poetry*, Garnett's *Cyclopaedia of English Literature*, The English Men of Letters Series, Quiller-Couch's *Shakespeare's Workmanship*.

Repeatedly, this Memorandum has emphasised the importance of reading contemporary literature; at no stage is this more important than in the last years of school life. How far it is possible to do it in school as a class subject must depend upon many circumstances, but in some way or other boys should be brought to some acquaintance with the greater living poets, dramatists, novelists. The library should have their works, or at least some of them, and if there is little or no opportunity of reading and discussing in class, then it must be done through the school societies already referred to.

The following are expressions of opinion on the scope and methods of Advanced Course work in English, by three members of the Committee:

" In the first year, a great deal of oral work would be needed to train the class in the principles of the subject as interpreted by the master. Most of the texts would need the master's comment and questioning all the way through, or at least part of the way. Questions on matter, style, and general criticism, together with imitative, suggested, or other artistic studies for the apter pupils, would be illuminated by a certain amount of lecturing on the periods as literary history. A suitable text is Dr Compton-

Rickett's *History*, published by Jack, 10s. 6d. The prime difficulty is to get the atmosphere, the work needing to be more philosophic than drily technical or subject-matterish. Too many school texts and 'Aids to Appreciation' abound in prosodical, analytical, and scientific details; the work wants to be more felt than analysed—of course, with discretion.

In the second year, critical questions are better answered, because the oppositions of style and thought in two periods already done teach contrast, comparison, and how to get at the characteristics of an age or a writer. This year, too, literary history might be read by the pupils themselves in private reading periods. Here the pupils have in each week seven periods with the master and three without. Something of the Dalton plan may be suitable —so much work being allotted per month. But Chaucer, and reading with the Science and Maths. pupils (thrice weekly) would still need to be orally conducted."

"As a subsidiary subject in an Advanced Course, English should be taken on general lines. My chief acquaintance in this matter is with boys who are taking a Science Course, and I find that they are rather apt to overlook the necessity for training in English when they begin to specialise on the scientific side. I have found it necessary to put before them specific reasons why—even for the sake of science—they should continue the study of English seriously. When they are attracted by this rather low motive of utility, it is usually possible to bring them to a love of literature for its own sake. The aim of the Course in English as a subsidiary subject should be an attempt at balance in the curriculum and a widening of interest, so that in later life boys may have literary interests as a relief from their specialised scientific occupations. For this reason, a course of Nineteenth Century literature seems to me most appropriate, a large number of works being read generally, none in minute detail."

"While agreeing with the opinion on the value of co-operation by other teachers throughout the school in developing powers of expression, I would strongly dissent from the apparent suggestion that essay work is less important in the Advanced Course than earlier, or than the reading and discussion of literature. On the contrary, I think it is indispensable, if a critical grasp of literature and increased power of thought are desirable, that boys at this stage should be given more time and opportunity for beating out and shaping their own judgments. The English master should regard the full-length essay—of University scholarship type— on literary and general subjects as the most valuable weapon in his armoury for this purpose, and should find more time than ever before for individual correction."

In drawing up this Memorandum the Committee has tried to avoid suggesting anything likely to stereotype the methods of teaching English; nowhere must there be greater variation than in Advanced Courses, inasmuch as the work in them is entrusted to highly qualified specialists who, by experience, have evolved methods suited to themselves and to the boys in their charge. Yet it is essential that the work should be inspired by a true conception of the aim in view and of the responsibility which rests upon the teacher. To this end the Departmental Report on the Teaching of English in England must never be forgotten as a source of inspiration and encouragement.

APPENDIX I

A SCHOOL DRAMATIC SOCIETY: ITS ORIGIN AND DEVELOPMENT

[*Note by the Revising Committee.*—The following account of the origin and development of a Dramatic Society in a London school was written in response to the special request of the Committee. It is probable that other schools throughout the country have had equal and perhaps greater success, yet to many others this record of actual achievement may prove both an inspiration and a practical guide.]

Most teachers will agree, we think, that the dramatic instinct is as deeply rooted in children as it is in the primitive savage who dramatises the very forces of nature and expresses his deepest emotions, whether religious or secular, by means of dramatic ceremonial. We all, indeed, make use, more or less according to our temperaments, of this dramatic instinct in teaching English or History or Modern Languages, but we do not perhaps sufficiently realise the powerful appeal that the dramatic method possesses or the deep subconscious sources that it can tap. Since the drama appeals to the emotions rather than to the intellect, it reaches that very common type of mind which feels the beauty of language and ideas only if the emotions are stirred and is indifferent to the appeal of logical exposition and analysis: the type of mind for which the printed page is dead until the magic of speech and gesture charm it into life and meaning. But the logical, mathematical type, too, is susceptible to the dramatic appeal and is broadened and humanised by giving heed to it. On general principles, then, there is room in our classes for the dramatic method.

It is not, however, our task to write on the drama in the classroom, but to set forth, as briefly as may be, the observed results of the foundation of a School Dramatic Society, and to show how those results have been obtained. The Dramatic Society of the school owes its creation to a School Pageant which the Headmaster initiated to celebrate the fiftieth anniversary of the erection of the present school buildings. It took the form of a series of short plays or episodes illustrating the history of the school from its foundation in the reign of Queen Elizabeth to the laying of the new foundation stone and the appointment of a Headmaster in 1873.

The plays were written by various members of the staff and produced by them, while the Pageant as a whole was put in charge of a master who saw to the costumes and properties, the school choir providing the incidental music. Since more than one hundred boys took part in the performances, it will be understood that the undertaking was ambitious and that inroads had to be made on the school time-table for rehearsals. The Pageant was a great success...and the General School results did not suffer!

The effect of the Pageant was to increase in the boys their respect for the school and its history, but results of much more universal application and therefore of greater significance were noted.

For instance, one point brought out was the great wealth of histrionic ability and the discovery of it in boys who had hitherto been classified as dull. Yet they were not dull on the stage, for they were able to interpret difficult rôles which made severe demands on the intelligence! We had judged them wrongly because we had not known how to appeal to their particular type of mind. Such boys as these seemed to blossom out in all directions after the Pageant and we could only conclude that, having found their vocation, they attacked their work with a new vigour and a new hope. The drama had irradiated their whole mental horizon.

A second observation we made was that the Pageant had created a team-spirit amongst the actors, singers, scene-shifters and producers which was comparable with that existing in the Cadet Corps or the cricket and football teams. The producers—all masters—came into intimate contact with the boys not as masters, or instructors, or trainers, but as part creators of a work of art—a very different relationship.

Lastly, it was found that there was an increased interest in the humanities and in the correct speaking of English. The scientists became interested in modern plays and abandoned their attitude of aloofness, whilst those who had acted in the Pageant were eager to act the plays studied in the classroom.

The Pageant indeed seemed to have stirred into action latent forces of great potency for good which we had not hitherto sufficiently utilised. When it was over, there was a feeling that something precious had gone out of the school life, and this feeling found expression in a petition from the older boys that a Dramatic Society should be founded. A meeting was called and, support from all quarters having been found, the Society came into being and a Committee of six was nominated. An entrance fee of 1s. and a subscription of 1s. per term were established on the principle that it is inherently wrong to give something for nothing. We found, however, that our profits were so large that we did not need the subscriptions and they were returned in the form of a reduction on the price of tickets to our performances.

In the first year of our existence we gave a one-act play at the Cadet Concert in December and an evening's entertainment in the Lent Term consisting of: A Latin Play; a scene from Shakespeare; a one-act tragedy written by a member of the staff; a musical sketch. Our net profits were some £20, which enabled us to present £5's worth of books on the drama to the Library and to set ourselves up in grease paint and other necessary equipment; moreover we had acquired valuable experience and shown that there was room in the school life for our Society.

In our second year, we determined to give two shows and to cast our net more widely to include in our sphere of action the smaller boys and thus train up our future members. The programme of our second entertainment consisted of: "The Mad Hatter's Tea Party," played by boys of 12; a Scene from *Twelfth Night*, played by boys of 14 to 15; *The Ghost of Jerry Bundler*, a thriller by W. W. Jacobs, played by boys of 16; "It All Depends," a farce by a member of the staff, played by boys of 16 and over. Next year we shall put in a French play in order to give the linguists a chance. Our profits were again in the neighbourhood of £20 and we were able to buy a set of new curtains, add books to the Library, and build a cupboard for storing costumes and properties.

When the Committee discussed the programme for the second show, it was found that there was a strong feeling that we should give *Arms and the Man*, which had already been read—after two or three rehearsals—to the Literary and Debating Society. The opportunity for an experiment was too good to be missed and we therefore agreed to *Arms and the Man* on the condition that it should be produced entirely without the help of any member of the staff. This suggestion was accepted with a readiness which was almost uncomplimentary, and rehearsals were started in the Christmas holidays. The result was startling: not only were the acting and the elocution better than in the plays produced by the staff, but the staging and the lighting were incomparably superior! We should like to stress this point strongly because we feel that we here touch the vital principles of School Dramatic Societies and the rôle that a master should play in them. The older boys must take the responsibility of organising the whole entertainment—printing tickets and programmes, seating, sale of tickets and refreshments, costumes and properties, producing and acting, and choosing and casting the play, etc.—and the master should take the younger boys in hand and train them to be able to undertake such responsibilities, keeping, of course, a general eye on all the activities of the Society. We will not elaborate this point here since its importance is evident.

We will conclude with a few practical points which may be of service to those who are interested in school Dramatic Societies and who have had no experience in connection with them.

The aim of a Dramatic Society should be to be self-sufficing as far as possible and to include in its activities the maximum number of boys. It is better therefore to give four short plays requiring twenty-four actors than one long play requiring six. Do not depend on outside help: thus, for making-up the actors pick out a boy with artistic ability and present him with a box of grease paints with the suggestion that he try his hands on his schoolfellows until he has learnt something of the capabilities of the art. It will be found that he will do the job extraordinarily well and become keenly interested in the work. When he is proficient get him to train a successor!

Costumes are a difficult problem: they are rather expensive to hire and there is sometimes difficulty in persuading mothers to make them for our actors. This difficulty, however, seems to vanish if the play is being produced by the boys themselves, no doubt because the producer is able to use pressure that would not be seemly in a master and because the boy feels that it is "up to him" to make the show a success. In general it is unwise to choose plays that require elaborate dressing, although, it must be admitted, costumes are very effective and a study of them will lead a boy into a charming bypath of historical research. A couple of boys interested in the subject can be appointed as costume experts and books on the subject can be bought for the Library out of profits.

Properties should be of the simplest kind and should be made in the workshop and the art room. A great deal can be done, for instance, with an ordinary chair and plywood if a throne is required. The art room can co-operate effectively in many ways and boys with artistic leanings can be employed in scene painting and poster designing.

Lighting is important and headlights should be installed if possible. This branch of our activities gives a chance to the boy of mechanical and scientific turn of mind, but if the voltage is heavy, his work will have to be supervised or accidents will occur.

We do most of our printing on the school press and are fortunate in that respect. As, however, a reasonably good press can be bought for about £12 there is no reason why a school should be without one. If there is a press, lino cuts can be used to decorate the programmes.

Criticisms of the performances of the Society should appear in the School Magazine, and it is wise to have them written by a boy with literary ability who may find it worth his while to study this branch of literature. Outside criticisms are valuable if informed, and as the British Drama League is willing to send critics to performances of its members, it is wise to join the League. Membership has the further advantage of opening the Library of the League to the members of the Society, and enough copies of a play can be borrowed to supply each character with a copy for rehearsals.

Every effort should be made to encourage boys to write plays for themselves. We have not yet produced a play written by one of our boys, but, if rumour is not lying, we are not far from this achievement. On the day when we see a play that has been written, produced, and acted by the boys, we shall feel that the Dramatic Society has really justified itself.

Music in the intervals is essential and hence some sort of an orchestra must be created if it does not already exist. The Dramatic Society thus extends a welcoming hand to a school activity which is perhaps somewhat neglected in this country.

The box-office arrangements give scope to boys of business ability who can tackle problems of organisation and publicity.

We hope we have said enough to show that a School Dramatic Society fulfils a useful function in school life and serves to correlate a large number of activities which would otherwise not be brought into contact.

APPENDIX II

A HOME READING SCHEME

The following scheme for School and Home Reading is supplementary to the literature course proper, which includes one book per term together with an anthology from which selected poems are learned by heart. There are also form libraries, the books for which are lent by the boys in the form, and which remain their own property. The scheme has developed from a plan introduced many years ago and has been working in its present form for four years in a large London school, receiving pupils from elementary schools into Shell form at the age of 11. These pass on to the III's, Lower IV's, Upper IV's, and V's, and from the Fifths they take the First School Examination. The scheme is also in practice below the Shell forms, though the lists of books are not given here. It should be added that the boys of each school year are classified as A, B, C, or D, according to the following plan. Those in *e.g.* III A are those of the best boys of their year who have elected to take Latin; III B consists of boys of equal standing who learn German; III C and III D do not learn any second foreign language, and include boys of less aptitude than those in III A, and III B.

Details of the working of the scheme are appended.

(*a*) The volumes included in the following lists are supplied *in duplicate* and two boys sitting together are thus reading the same book.

(*b*) The books are changed fortnightly, each boy thus having an opportunity of reading seventeen or eighteen books during a school year. As the scheme includes four years of the boy's school life, he has been put in the way of reading seventy or more standard works of English literature. (Boys in Lower, Middle, and Upper V take the First School Examination, and are not included in the scheme: those of V Remove do not sit for the examination and are so included.)

(*c*) The volumes in each form include works of varied character and somewhat varied difficulty; many of them are books of selections. Books are "tried out," and volumes are added, withdrawn, or interchanged, at the suggestion of the English Master, the Form Master, or the boys.

(*d*) Interest in the books is stimulated by the English Master's talk with groups who have read a particular book, and by the knowledge that the school terminal examination will include a question on the books read during the term. The discussion of the books is limited, as a rule, to one period per fortnight, and preferably that period in which the books are changed. Boys not concerned in the discussion are meanwhile reading their Home Reading books silently.

(*e*) As a rule, the books selected for A and B forms are of greater difficulty than those for the C and D. Each list contains also books studied in the class of the same grade if not included in the syllabus for a particular class; there are also found in some cases books which were studied in detail in a previous class.

(*f*) Apart from its ultimate cultural value the scheme serves the immediate purpose of providing a large background of works read by the time of the First School Examination year.

FORM ORGANISATION

Age group				
11–12	Shell A	Shell B	Shell C	Shell D
12–13	III A	III B	III C	III D
13–14	Lower IV A	Lower IV B	Lower IV C	Lower IV D
14–15	Upper IV A	Upper IV B	Upper IV C	Upper IV D
15–16	—	—	—	V Remove

LISTS OF BOOKS READ IN THE ABOVE FORMS

Shell A (11–12)

Ballads and Ballad Poems.
The Chimes.
Rip Van Winkle.
Parables from Nature.
Lamb and Shakespeare.
Ancient Mariner.
Faerie Queene (simplified).
Form Room Plays (Junior).
Animal Stories.

Fort Amity.
Stories from History. Pt I.
The White Company.
Longer Narrative Poems.
Don Quixote.
Gulliver's Travels.
The Younger Characters of Dickens.
Birds and Beasts.

III A (12–13)

Lays of Ancient Rome.
Sketch Book.
Romany Rye.
Junior Modern Poetry.
Stories from Hakluyt.
History of a Candle.
Essays of Elia.
As You Like It.
Silas Marner.
Selected Stories from "Q."

Junior Modern Prose.
The Tempest.
Henry IV.
Natural History of Selborne.
Life and Death of Jason.
Tales of a Grandfather.
Wreck of the "Golden Mary."
The Canterbury Pilgrims.
Clarendon: Cavalier and Roundhead.

Lower IV A (13–14)

Bible in Spain.
Hugh Walpole, Anthology.
Harold.
Childe Harold's Pilgrimage.
Goldsmith's Poems.
Macaulay's Third Chapter.
Vicar of Wakefield.
Form Room Plays (Senior).
Life of Goldsmith.
Keats (Selections).

Plutarch's Lives.
English Lyrical Verse.
Wars with the Turks.
William the Silent.
Moby Dick.
Letters from High Latitudes.
Humphrey Clinker (Selections).
A Lady's Life in the Rocky Mountains.

Upper IV A (14–15)

Motley's Dutch Republic.
Belloc, French Revolution.
Selections from Pope.
Modern Essays from "The Times."
Literature and Labour.

Essay on Clive.
Macaulay's Essay on Hampden.
Modern Essays (King's Treasuries).
"Alpha of the Plough": Essays.

Sohrab and Rustum.
Dryden's Prose (Selected).
Macaulay's Johnson.
Chaucer's Prologue.
Selected English Essays.
Hamlet.
Henry VIII.

Shelley and Keats.
English Mail Coach.
Heroes and Hero Worship.
Shakespeare's Characters.
Sense and Sensibility.
Earlier English Drama.

Shell B (11–12)

Ancient Mariner.
Merchant of Venice.
The Bee.
Reynard the Fox.
Longfellow (Selections).
The Cricket on the Hearth.
English Admirals.
A Midsummer Night's Dream.
Birds in a Village.
Natural History of Selborne.
The Old Post.

The Heroes.
The Eye Witness.
Tales of a Wayside Inn.
Marmion.
Animal Stories.
The King of the Golden River.
Trelawny.
Don Quixote.
Wild Life Studies.
Gulliver's Travels.

III B (12–13)

Cloister and the Hearth.
Twelfth Night.
Lighter Prose.
Lavengro.
Sports and Pastimes in English
  Literature.
Tales from Tolstoy.
Lorna Doone.
Roll Call of Honour.
Henry IV, Pt I.

Tales of Travel.
Atalanta's Race.
Silas Marner.
Tales of a Grandfather.
Pages from Latin Authors.
Evangeline.
Plays before Shakespeare.
In the Morning of Time.
Junior Modern Prose.
As You Like It.

Lower IV B (13–14)

De Coverley Papers.
Book of Story Poems.
Narratives from Macaulay.
English Admirals.
Macaulay's Second Chapter.
Childe Harold's Pilgrimage.
Lore of the Wanderer.
Embassy to the Great Mogul.
Prose and Poetry (Newbolt).
The Task.

The Ancient Mariner.
Conquest of Peru.
Parables from Nature.
Last Days of Pompeii.
London in Literature.
Eöthen.
Thomas of Reading.
Tales from Boccaccio.
Alva (Motley).
She Stoops to Conquer.

Upper IV B (14–15)

Macaulay's Hampden.
Paradise Lost (V and VI).
Paston Letters.
At Home and Abroad.
Comus.
Cottar's Saturday Night.
Gibbon's Constantinople.
De Quincey.
Maria Edgeworth.
Macaulay's Addison.
Heroes and Hero Worship.
Modern Essays (ed. Sampson).
Macaulay's Warren Hastings.

Pioneers of France in the New
  World.
Morte D'Arthur.
Hamlet.
Boswell and Johnson in the
  Hebrides.
An Inland Voyage.
Historical Portraits in English
  Literature.
Nine Modern Plays.
Josephus.
Selections from Browning.

Shell C (11–12)

The Lay of the Last Minstrel.
Ivanhoe.
The Lord of the Isles.
Longer Narrative Poems.
Christmas Carol.
Tanglewood Tales.
Gulliver's Travels.
Robinson Crusoe.
Letters to my Grandson.

Story of the Iliad.
Don Quixote.
Morte D'Arthur.
Wonder Book.
Animal Stories.
The King of the Golden River.
Stories from History.
Little Men.
Little Women.

III C (12–13)

Selected Stories by "Q."
The Gospel Story.
Tales of a Wayside Inn.
Lay of the Last Minstrel.
Fort Amity.
As You Like It.
Lighter Verse.
Cruise of the "Cachelot."
The Wonder Book.
The Canterbury Pilgrims.

Sohrab and Rustum.
Lucian's Trips to Wonder-
  land.
Black Beauty.
Feats on the Fiord.
Readings from Borrow.
Voyages of Columbus.
The Heroes.
Pattern Poetry (I).

Lower IV C (13–14)

History of Virginia.
Mungo Park's Travels.
Addison's Prose.
Cranford.
Voyages to Japan.
Rural Rides.
Ships and Seamen.
Evergreen Stories.

English Diarists.
Pattern Poetry (II).
Castle Rackrent.
Evangeline.
Siege of Syracuse.
Life of Julius Caesar.
Lives of Brutus and Corio-
  lanus.

Upper IV C (14–15)

"Alpha of the Plough": Essays.
Pages of History.
Macbeth.
Life of Wolsey.
Essays by Robert Lynd.
Selections from Borrow.
,,   Malory.
,,   Froissart.
,,   Kinglake.

Keats's Isabella and the Eve of St Agnes.
Macaulay's Life of Bunyan.
Macaulay's Essay on Bunyan.
Hugh Walpole, Anthology.
The Rivals.
Goldsmith's Prose and Poems.
English Mail Coach.
Lay of the Last Minstrel.
Sohrab and Rustum.

Shell D (11–12)

Horatius, etc.
Adventures of Odysseus.
Water Babies.
Robinson Crusoe.
Song of Beowulf.
Pilgrim's Progress.
Don Quixote.
Christmas Carol.

Wonder Book.
Tanglewood Tales.
The Bee.
Jackanapes.
Pied Piper.
Evergreen Stories.
Hiawatha.

III D (12–13)

The Forsaken Merman (and other poems).
Tales of Travel.
The Fight for Peace.
Scott's Last Expedition.
Swiss Family Robinson.
Sohrab and Rustum.
Ingoldsby Legends.
Book of Golden Deeds.

Hiawatha.
The Gold Bug.
Robinson Crusoe.
Pilgrim's Progress.
Trelawny.
Christmas Carol.
Toilers of the Sea.
Survey of London.
Uncle Tom's Cabin.

Lower IV D (13–14)

Tale of Two Cities.
Stories from History.
Tower of London.
Cranford.
Anson's Voyages.
Hakluyt.
Livingstone's Travels.
Captain Singleton.
Christmas Carol.

Toilers of the Sea.
Vicar of Wakefield.
Last Days of Pompeii.
Evangeline, etc.
Last of the Mohicans.
Discovery of Guiana.
Montezuma (Prescott).
Junior Modern Essays.

Upper IV D (14–15)

Under the Greenwood Tree.
She Stoops to Conquer.
Quentin Durward.
Great Expectations.
Maid Marian.
Journal of the Plague.
Sketches by Modern Writers.
Pages of Science.

Henry VIII.
The Morning of Time.
The Life of Nelson.
Youth.
Sohrab and Rustum.
Prose for Repetition.
Romany Rye.

V Remove (15–16)

Macaulay's Clive.
Selections from Burns.
King Lear.
The "Autocrat" Series.
The Mill on the Floss.
Hamlet.
The Wonder Book.
Standard Prose (Kings Treasuries).
Master Historians.
Story and Rhyme.
English Letters.

Narratives from Gibbon's Roman Empire.
The Beau of Bath.
Abbot Samson.
The Rivals.
Napier's Battles—Salamanca and Corunna.
Pepys's Diary (Selections).
Black Hole of Calcutta.
Wars with the Turks.
Natural History of Selborne.

APPENDIX III

THE REPORT OF THE JOINT COMMITTEE ON GRAMMATICAL TERMINOLOGY

With regard to the Report of the Joint Committee on Grammatical Terminology, there is the fullest recognition of the advantages of a common terminology for all languages; indeed many corresponding members declined to offer any criticism on this very ground, that the advantages are so great that it is not worth while to differ on points of detail, while others who felt very strongly opposed to the use of classical case names in English were ready to accept them for the same reason. At the same time there is a marked feeling that classical necessities and usages have had a preponderating influence in shaping the decisions of the Joint Committee.

The following criticisms were agreed to:

1. The classification of sentences into simple, complex, double, multiple does not include all possible forms of sentence, *e.g.* The man took off his hat and the servant hung it on the peg which was behind the door.

2. The term "predicative adjective" had better be "adjective used predicatively" (cf. verb used transitively). Similarly the term "epithet noun" is unnecessary; for other parts of speech than nouns can be used as adjectives.

3. In English the accusative and infinitive construction should never be termed a clause, which should contain a finite verb.

4. The term "clause of comparison" should be dropped, and the clause of manner and the clause of degree be treated as different kinds of adverbial clauses.

5. The use of such terms as "if clause," "then clause" is unnecessary in English; it is an example of the classical elaboration referred to above.

6. Such words as "when," "where," etc., introducing subordinate clauses (even when they are dependent questions) should in English be called conjunctions and not adverbs.

7. The words Present, Past, Future, should be kept as the names of *time* groups, and other qualifying words added to indicate the exact tense, *e.g.*

	Present	Past	Future
Indefinite	I write	I wrote	I shall write
Continuous	I am writing	I was writing	I shall be writing
Perfect	I have written	I had written	I shall have written

The terms "future in the past" for "I should write" and "future perfect in the past" for "I should have written" are cumbersome, but as satisfactory as any alternative.

8. Just as the noun in the subject is called the subject word, so the finite verb in the predicate should be called the predicate verb.

APPENDIX IV

BIBLIOGRAPHY

While much time and care have been given to the preparation of this bibliography, it is possible that many good and useful books are not included. Those mentioned have been either examined by the Revising Committee or specially recommended by corresponding members.

The Revising Committee recommends that the list of books tabulated according to age-suitability be read (especially in Literature) *in conjunction with the separate lists of books published in Series and of editions of Shakespeare's plays.* The bibliography will thus be found less incomplete than at first sight it may appear.

Recent experience shows that prices of books have changed considerably and will probably do so in the future. The prices given below have been obtained, as far as possible, from up-to-date catalogues. The members of the Revising Committee would like to express their appreciation of the willing co-operation of the various publishers, both in sending books for inspection and in assisting in the matter of price reference.

GRAMMAR AND COMPOSITION

A. Up to Age of 11

Grammar.

Geo. Sampson. Cambridge Lessons in English, Book I. Cambridge University Press. 1s. 6d.

Palser and Lewis. Junior Outline Grammar of Function. Harrap. 1s.
Very good; on absolutely modern lines.

Palser and Lewis. Graduated Exercises in English Grammar and Composition. Harrap. 1s.
Companion to the above; but can be used separately.

E. Benson. Junior Course in Grammar. Dent. 1s. 6d.
Clearly printed. Based on passages for study.

Grammar and Composition.

Wilson. English Spoken and Written. Part I. Nelson. 1s. 6d.

Twentyman. English Grammar and Composition. Part I. Rivington. 1s. 6d.
Well graded and on modern lines.

Rahtz. Preliminary English. Methuen. 2s. 3d.
> *On sound modern lines by an experienced teacher.*

Collins's New World English Course. Book I. 1s. 2d.
> *Mainly composition and very attractively produced.*

Morgan. Groundwork of English. Murray, Parts I and II. 1s. 6d. each.
> *Recommended by correspondents.*

Composition.

Marriott. A Junior Course of English. Parts I and II. Harrap. 1s. each.

Kenny. Exercises in Composition. 3 parts. Arnold. 5d. each.
> *Very useful where no text-book is possible.*

Black's Picture Lessons in English. 1s.

Marsh. Picture Compositions. Parts I, II, III. Blackie. 10d. each.
> *All well done.*

Evans Bros. Pictures and Chats about Animals. 6d. Teacher's edition at 2s. 6d.
> *Excellent in every way for early compositions.*

B. Ages 11–14

Grammar.

Palser and Lewis. Junior Outline Grammar of Function. Harrap. 1s.

Palser and Lewis. Graduated Exercises in English Grammar and Composition. Harrap. 1s.
> *Companion to the above; but can be used separately.*

Palser and Lewis. A New Outline Grammar of Function. Harrap. 1s. 6d.
> *Modern lines; sound; well printed.*

Geo. Sampson. Cambridge Lessons in English. Book II, 1s. 10d. Book III, 2s. 6d. Cambridge Univ. Press.

Morgan. A Preparatory English Grammar. Harrap. 2s.
> *Very full treatment of preparatory English grammar.*

Catnach. A New Grammar Book. Blackie. 2s. 6d.
> *On modern lines.*

Smith and Ball. English Grammar. Mills and Boon. 2s.

Smith and Ball. English Composition. Mills and Boon. 1s. 6d.
> *Companion books by practical teachers; mainly graded exercises.*

Grammar and Composition.

Wilson. English Spoken and Written. Part II, 1s. 6d. Part III, 1s. 9d. Nelson.

Treble and Vallins. Gateway to English. Parts I, II, and III. 2s. each. Oxford Univ. Press.
> *Well printed; illustrated; well graded for elementary stages.*

Marsh and Goodman. A Junior Course of English Grammar and Composition. Parts I and II. 2s. 3d. each. Blackie.
> *Much detail and plenty of exercises.*

Twentyman. English Grammar and Composition. Part II. 2s.
> *Continuation of Part I on similar lines.*

Rahtz. Junior English. Methuen. 2s. 3d.
> *Continues the Preliminary English.*

Collins's New World English Course. Book II, 1s. 2d. Book III, 1s. 3d.

Marriott. A Year's Work in English. Harrap. 2s. 3d.
> *Recommended by many teachers. On very modern lines.*

Bewsher. Exercises in English. Bell. 1s. 9d.
> *Exercises only. Suitable for boys 13–14.*

Campbell. Lower English. Blackie. Limp cloth. 1s. 6d.

Albert. A Practical Course in Intermediate English. Harrap. 2s. 6d.
> *Well-chosen exercises.*

Kenny. English Composition. University of London Press. 2s. 6d.

Composition.

Jepson. The Writer's Craft. Dent. 2s.

Nelson's Pattern Plays, and Play Making. 1s. 6d.

Kenny. Composition from English Models. Book I, 1s. 6d. Book II, 2s. 6d. Arnold.

Fowler. English Exercises. Part I. Macmillan. 2s. 6d.
> *A well-graded scheme.*

Guy Boas. New English Exercises. Arnold. 2s.
> *Very good introduction to the various forms of composition.*

Pritchard. Intermediate English Extracts and Exercises. Harrap. 2s. 6d.

Kenny. Junior English Composition. Arnold. 2s.
> *Used by many teachers.*

Kenny. Composition from English Models. Book I, 1s. 6d. Book II, 2s. 6d. Arnold.

Bendall. Graduated Exercises in English Composition. Blackie. 1s. 6d.
> *Useful for additional exercises.*

Winbolt. Course of English Composition. Blackie. 2s. 6d.

Fowler. First Course of Essay Writing. Black. 8d.
> *Well arranged and bound.*

Smith and Ball. English Composition. Mills and Boon. 1s. 6d.
Cruse. English Composition. Oxford Univ. Press. 2s. 6d.
Well graded. Based on the study of literary models.

Pocock. Précis Writing for Beginners. Blackie. 2s. 6d.

C. AGES 14–16

Grammar.

Gratton and Gurrey. Our Living Language. Nelson. 3s. 6d.
Arnold Smith. Grammar and the Use of Words. Methuen. 3s.
Mason. New English Grammar. (Ashton.) Bell. 4s. 6d.
A sound grammar on historical lines.

Morgan and Treble. Senior English Grammar (with chapters on Vocabulary and Phonetics). Murray. 3s. 6d.

Grammar and Composition.

Rahtz. Higher English. Methuen. 5s.
Admirable in preparation for First School Examinations.

Bate. English Composition. Bell. 4s. 6d.
Much wider than suggested by the name; a complete course up to First School Examination standard. Many well-chosen exercises.

Nesfield. Matriculation Course. Macmillan. 4s.
Excellent exercises.

Morgan and Lattimer. A Higher Course of English Practice. Murray. 3s. 6d.
A thoroughly practical book, based on examining experience.

Composition.

Murison. English Composition. Cambridge Univ. Press. 6s.
Sound and scholarly: well deserving of special mention.

Hammond. Progressive Exercises in English Composition. Oxford Univ. Press. 3s. 6d.
Hammond. An Introduction to English Composition. Oxford Univ. Press. 3s. 6d.
Fowler. English Exercises. Part II. Macmillan. 3s. 6d.
A well-graded scheme.

D'Oyley. Composition from English Models. Arnold. 2s. 6d.
Fowler. English Essays. Macmillan. 1s. 9d.
English Spoken and Written. Part IV. Nelson. 2s.
Précis, Notes, and Summaries. Nelson. 1s. 9d.
Compton. A Systematic Course of Précis Writing. Harrap. 2s. 6d.
A well-arranged, systematic, common-sense course.

Williams. Progressive Précis and Paraphrase. Methuen. 2s. 6d.
Bradshaw and Phillips. Selected Passages for Précis Writing. Bell. 2s. 6d.
Prose for Précis. Dent. 1s. 4d.
Further Prose for Précis. Dent. 1s. 4d.
Fowler. King's English (abridged). Oxford Univ. Press. 3s.
Winbolt. Matriculation Précis. Bell. 1s. 6d.
Robeson. Progressive Course of Précis Writing. Oxford Univ. Press. 2s. 6d.
> *Well graded and on right lines.*

Ready. Present Day Précis. Bell. 2s. 6d.
> *Especially for students who require advanced précis work.*

Latter. Progressive Précis Writing. Blackie. 3s. 6d.
Palser. A Practical Course of Précis Writing. Part II. University of London Press. 1s. 10d. and 2s.

LITERATURE

D. Up to the Age of 11

Prose Texts.

Prose Texts for Junior Forms. Horace Marshall. 1s.
> (*Many standard books*, e.g. *Pilgrim's Progress, Coverley Papers, etc.*)

Bell's Short English Texts. *E.g.* Tanglewood Tales: Wonder Book. 10d. to 1s.

Verse Anthologies.

Jagger. A Book of English Poems. Introd. Part [Illustrated]. Univ. of London Press. 1s. 3d.
Frank Jones. The Golden Book of Children's Verse. Blackie. 2s. 3d.
J. C. Smith. A Book of Verse for Boys and Girls. Part I. Oxford Univ. Press. 1s. 4d. 1s. 8d. cloth.
> *Used in many schools as an anthology.*

Kenneth Grahame. Cambridge Book of Verse for Children. 2 parts. Cambridge Univ. Press. 2s. 6d. each.
> *Well bound and printed. A wide selection.*

C. L. Thomson. A Book of Ballads. Horace Marshall. 2s. 3d.
> *Well selected—right down to modern times.*

Arnold. Junior Poetry. 1s. 2d.
> *A good selection at a moderate price.*

A Treasury of Verse for School and Home. 4 books. Harrap. Limp cloth, 1s. 3d. to 1s. 9d.
> *Well chosen.*

The Carfax Book of English Verse. [See Note under *Series.*]

Readers and Miscellaneous.

Charles. Introduction to English Course. Books I and II. Collins. 1s. each.

De Sélincourt. The Way of Literature. Book I, 1s. 8d. Book II, 1s. 9d. Book III, 2s. Collins.

The Haliburton Fifth Reader. Harrap. 2s. 6d.

The Fairy Book, Book I. Nelson. 1s. 3d.

The Water Babies. Nelson. 1s. 3d.

The Flying Trunk and other stories. Nelson. 1s. 3d.

The Adventures of Don Quixote. Nelson. 1s. 3d.

Andersen and Grimm. Nelson. 1s. 6d.

Tales from the Arabian Nights. Nelson. 1s. 6d.

Untold Tales of the Past. Dent. 1s.

Old Gold: A Book of Fables and Parables. Dent. 1s.

Marshall's Temple Readers. 2s. 6d. to 3s. Good extracts.

Black's Sentinel Readers (Speight). Book VI. 2s. to 3s.
> *Extracts chosen on lines recommended in the Report, some quite modern.*

Headland and Treble. A Dramatic Reader, I, II. Oxford Univ. Press. 2s. each.
> *An excellent introduction to drama.*

The Story Teller's Hall. Prose and Poetry. Dent. 2s. 6d.

Elizabeth Lee. Selections from English Literature. Arnold. 2s. 6d.
> *Recommended by correspondents.*

Thomas. Norse Tales. Oxford Univ. Press. 2s. 6d.
> *Well chosen and printed.*

E. AGES 11–14

Prose Anthologies.

Humour of To-day. Harrap. 2s. 6d.

Lighter English Prose. Dent. 1s. 4d.

Bible Anthology. Dent. 1s. 4d.

Junior Modern Essays. Dent. 1s. 4d.

Prose Texts.

The Song of Beowulf. Dent. 1s. [See also *Series* Section.]

Verse Anthologies.

Alice Meynell. The School of Poetry. Collins. 2s. 6d. Also in 3 graded parts, 10d., 10d., 1s. 3d. each.

Hall. Selections from English Poets. Books I and II. Harrap. 1s. 3d. each.

Edgar and Chilman. A Treasury of Verse. Harrap. 2s. 6d.

Jones. Golden Book of Narrative Verse. Blackie. 2s. 3d.

Poems and Ballads of Scottish History. Blackie. 1s. 6d.
Jagger. A Book of English Poems. Univ. of London Press. Part I, 1s. 6d. Part II, 1s. 6d.
Pattern Poetry. Part I, 1s. 6d. Part II, 1s. 9d. Nelson.
English Lyrical Verse. Dent. 1s. 4d.
Junior Modern Poetry. Dent. 1s. 4d.
A Book of Lighter Verse. Dent. 1s. 4d.
A Treasury of Verse for School and Home. Four books. Harrap. Limp cloth. 1s. 3d. to 1s. 9d.
Arnold. English Ballads. Edited by Newbolt. Limp cloth, 2s. 6d. English Narrative Poems. Edited by Newbolt. Limp cloth, 2s. 6d.
>*A fine collection.*

J. C. Smith. A Book of Verse for Boys and Girls. Part II, 1s. 4d., cloth 1s. 8d. Part III, 2s. 6d., cloth 3s. Oxford Univ. Press.
>*Considered by many the best anthology for schools.*

Ridges. Poetica. Blackie. 2s. 6d.
>*A well-graded anthology.*

John Drinkwater. The Way of Poetry. Collins. 2s. 6d., or in 4 books, 1s. each.
>*Excellent.*

Wilson. Coronata. Dent. 2s. 6d.
>*Excellently prepared and set out.*

The Carfax Book of English Verse. [See Note under *Series*.]

Drama.

One-Act Plays of To-day. 1st, 2nd and 3rd Series. Harrap. 2s. 6d. each.
Selections from English Dramatists. Harrap. 2s. 6d.
Little Plays from Shakespeare. Nelson. (1st and 2nd Series.) 1s. 9d. each.
A Dramatic Reader. (Headland and Treble.) Vol. III. Oxford Univ. Press. 2s. 6d.

Readers and Miscellaneous.

Kenneth Grahame. The Wind in the Willows. Methuen. 1s. 6d.
>*Good animal stories.*

Guy Boas. Humorous Narratives. Arnold. 2s. 6d.
The Lure of the Sea. Harrap. 2s. 6d.
By-gone England. Harrap. 2s. 6d.
The Scott Book. Bell. 2s. 6d.
Chappell. The Threshold of Literature. Dent. 2s. 6d.
Fabre's Book of Insects. Nelson. 1s. 6d.
The Roll Call of Honour. Nelson. 1s. 9d.
John Buchan. The Path of the King. Nelson. 1s. 9d.

John Buchan. Prester John. Nelson. 1s. 6d.
W. W. Jacobs. Fifteen Stories. Methuen. 1s. 6d.
Birmingham. Spanish Gold. Methuen. 1s. 6d.
Graded Bible Readers. Nelson. 1s. 6d. to 3s. 6d.
        Suitable from junior forms to the middle school.

Wilson. Treasure Trove. Illustrated. Dent. 2s. 6d.
        *Excellent collection of prose and poetry. Would do for
        older boys too.*

Francillon. Gods and Heroes. Ginn. 3s. 6d.
        Well bound and printed.

Arnold. Chips from a Bookshelf. 2s. 6d.
Arnold. In Golden Realms. 2s. 6d.
        *Both give extracts of good length and wide choice of
        author and subject.*

Hudson. Representative Passages from English Literature.
    Bell. 3s. 6d.
        Well chosen.

Cambridge Readings in Literature. Edited by George Sampson.
        *An excellent work. There are five books graded to suit
        children from 12 upwards. 3s. to 4s. Books I and II
        are also divided into parts, each 2s.*

Highroads to Literature. Nelson. 2s. to 3s. 6d.
        A graded series of books containing well-chosen extracts.

F. Ages 14–16

Prose Anthologies.

Partridge. A Book of English Prose, 1700–1914. Arnold. 2s. 6d.
Fowler. A Book of English Prose, 1470–1900. Macmillan. 2s. 6d.
        Well-chosen selection from the great prose writers.

Narrative Essays and Sketches. Harrap. 2s. 6d.
Newbolt. Essays and Essayists. Nelson. 1s. 9d.
D'Oyley. English Essays. Arnold. 2s. 6d.
Essays of Modern Masters. Methuen. 1s. 6d.
Essays of To-day. Harrap. 2s. 6d.
Modern Essays. Dent. 1s. 4d.
Short Stories of To-day. Harrap. 2s. 6d.
Elias. English Literature in Prose and Verse. Vols. III–IV.
    Harrap. 2s. each.
        An attractive collection.
                    [See also *Series* Section.]

Prose Texts.

Sleight. Goldsmith's Essays. Harrap. 2s. 6d.
Bailey. A Shorter Boswell. Nelson. 1s. 9d.

Verse Anthologies.

Hall. Selections from English Poets. Books III and IV. Harrap. 1s. 6d. each.

The Queen's Treasures Book of Verse. Bell. 3s. 6d.

The Golden Book of Modern English Poetry. Dent. 2s. 6d.

Pattern Poetry. Part III. Nelson. 1s. 9d.

Mount Helicon. Arnold. 2s. 6d.
> *A very complete anthology, which might be kept throughout the school career.*

J. C. Smith. A Book of Verse for Boys and Girls. Part III. Oxford Univ. Press. 3s.

Ridges. Poetica. Blackie. 2s. 6d.

Palgrave. Golden Treasury. Macmillan, 3s. 6d.; and Oxford Univ. Press, 2s.

Poems of To-day. First and Second Series. Sidgwick and Jackson. 2s. each.
> *An anthology compiled by the English Association.*

An Anthology of Modern Verse. Methuen. 2s. 6d. With Notes, 3s.
> *Admirably chosen.*

John Drinkwater. The Way of Poetry. Collins. 2s. 6d.

Dixon and Grierson. The English Parnassus. Oxford Univ. Press. 6s. 6d.
> *Very complete anthology from Chaucer to Matthew Arnold.*

Jagger. A Book of English Poems. Univ. of London Press. Part III, 2s. Part IV, 2s. 3d.

Drama.

Selected Plays of Shakespeare. (Nine in one volume.) Dent. 1s. 10d.

Early English Drama. Nelson. 1s. 9d.

Nine Modern Plays. Nelson. 1s. 9d.

The Shoemaker's Holiday. Dent. 1s.

She Stoops to Conquer. Dent. 1s. 4d.

The Rivals. Dent. 1s. 4d.

The Knight of the Burning Pestle. Blackie's Plain Texts. 1s.

Plays Before Shakespeare. Dent. 1s. 4d.

Milestones and The Great Adventure. Methuen. 1s. 6d.

One-Act Plays of To-day. 1st, 2nd, and 3rd Series. Harrap. 2s. 6d. each.

Readers and Miscellaneous.

Taylor. Words and Places. Nelson. 1s. 9d.

The Pleasant Land of England. Nelson. 1s. 9d.

Scott. The Man and the Book. Nelson. 1s. 9d

Selections from the Prose of Thomas Carlyle. Marshall. 2s.
Selections from the Prose of John Ruskin. Marshall. 2s.
Four Stories by Conrad. Dent. 1s. 4d.
Alpha of the Plough. 1st and 2nd Series. 1s. 4d. each.
Cambridge Readings in Literature. Edited by George Sampson.
    3s. to 4s.
Modern Essays from "The Times." Arnold. 2s. 6d.
> *A collection of the concluding articles on the leader page.
> Most useful for those who want modern prose.*

G. Series. (For Various Ages)

The Kings Treasuries of English Literature. Dent. 1s. 4d.
    [A few at 1s.]
The Teaching of English Series. Nelson. Most, 1s. 9d. Many,
    1s. 6d.
Macmillan's English Literature Series for Schools. 1s., 2s. 6d.
> *These three series stand alone in range, format and excel-
> lence of choice. Some of these books have already been
> mentioned under sub-headings; many others are equally
> good. For further details see publishers' catalogues.*

Poetry and Life Series. Harrap. 1s. 6d.
> *Cheap, but well-printed series of English poets. The man
> and his poetry.*

"Q." The Englishman Series. Dent. 2s.
Everyman's Library Series. Dent. 2s.
The Carfax Book of English Verse. Sidgwick and Jackson.
    10d. to 2s. each.
> *These eight volumes, forming a graded series for all
> ages, together with "The Approach to Poetry," are
> well chosen and attractively produced.*

John Drinkwater Series. Collins Clear Type Press. 6d. to 1s.
Socrates Booklets Series. Black. 1s. Cloth 1s. 3d.
Moorhouse. The Ring of Words. Dent. 1s. 6d. to 2s. 3d.
> *Three volumes. A full anthology.*

The Way of Literature Series. Collins Clear Type Press. 1s. 8d.
    to 2s. 9d.
> *Six excellently printed volumes.*

Prose Texts for Junior Forms. Horace Marshall. 1s.
Bell's Short English Texts. 10d. to 1s.
Riverside Literature Series. Harrap. 1s. 6d. to 3s. 6d.
> *A wide range, well produced, good introductions.*

Longman's Class Books of English Literature. Limp cloth. 1s. 9d.
> *Well produced, a wide range including Sohrab and Rustum,
> many of Scott's novels (abridged), Micah Clarke (un-
> abridged), Morris's Sigurd the Volsung, etc., etc.*

Oxford Select English Classics. Limp cloth. 6d. each.
> *This excellently printed series covers a wide field of poetry and prose.*

Bell's English Texts for Secondary Schools. 1s. to 1s. 6d.
> *A most useful series, edited by competent scholars who usually adopt the comparative method, e.g. Guthkelch— Lamb's Letters and Essays, and Bate's King Arthur (Malory and Tennyson).*

Standard English Classics. Ginn. 2s. 3d. to 4s. 6d.
> *Admirably produced, sensible introduction and notes.*

Cambridge English Literature for Schools. 1s. 3d. to 3s. 6d.
> *Many standard texts.*

English Texts. Edited by Rouse. Blackie. Limp cloth. 10d.
> *Well printed. Wide range.*

Blackie's Smaller English Classics. Limp cloth. 6d.
> *Well printed.*

Arnold's Laureate Poetry Books. 8d.
> *Well printed.*

Heath's English Classics. Harrap. 6d. to 2s. 6d.
> *Well produced; good notes.*

Cambridge Plain Texts. 1s. 3d.
> *Excellently printed and produced.*

Bohn's Popular Library. Bell. 2s.
> *Too well known to need comment.*

World's Classics. Oxford. 2s.
> *The widest possible range. Note especially Six Plays by Contemporaries of Shakespeare.*

Methuen's English Classics. Limp cloth. 1s. 6d. to 2s.

Clarendon Series of English Literature. Clarendon Press. 3s. 6d.
> *E.g. Cowper: Introduction; essays by Bagehot and Hazlitt; selections. Many writers dealt with on this plan.*

Collins's Illustrated School Classics. 1s. 6d. to 2s.

Collins's Illustrated Pocket Classics. 2s.

Oxford Standard Authors (including Poets). 3s. 6d.

Oxford Plain Texts. 1s. to 1s. 6d.

Murray's Modern English Series. 1s. 9d.

The London Series of English Texts. Univ. of London Press. [Ed. by Allardyce Nicoll.] 1s. 9d. to 3s.

EDITIONS OF SHAKESPEARE

It is the opinion of the Committee that where notes are given, they had better be either foot-notes or marginal notes, not relegated to the end of the book.

New Hudson Shakespeare. Ginn. 2s. 6d.
> *Excellent introduction, foot-notes, careful text, glossarial index. Quotations from Sources.*

Methuen's Shakespeare. (Methuen's English Classics.) Limp cloth, 1s. 6d.
> *Excellent introduction, notes at the end.*

Plays of Shakespeare edited by G. S. Gordon. Oxford Univ. Press. 2s. each. Limp cloth or boards.
> *Good introduction, notes at end.*

Arden Shakespeare. Methuen. 6s.
> *Well bound and printed. Good introduction and notes.*

Heath's Shakespeare. Harrap. 2s. 6d.
> *Very good notes.*

Warwick Shakespeare. Blackie. 2s. 6d.
> *Well bound, excellent notes.*

Carmelite Shakespeare. Horace Marshall. Limp cloth. 1s. 3d. to 1s. 6d.
> *Good notes and printing.*

Oxford and Cambridge Shakespeare. Gill. 2s. 3d., 3s. 3d.
> *A much used series.*

Academy Shakespeare. Chambers. 1s. 6d.
> *Very sound introduction, notes at the end.*

Plain Texts. Blackie's Plain Text Shakespeare. 6d.
Plain Texts. Oxford Plain Text Shakespeare. 1s.
Plain Texts. Chambers's Plain Text Shakespeare. 9d.
> *All well produced.*

Bell's Shakespeare for Schools. 1s. 9d.
Blackie's Junior School Shakespeare. 1s. 3d.
The Teaching of English Series. Nelson. 1s. 9d.
Kings Treasuries Series. Dent. 1s. and 1s. 4d.
Touchstone Shakespeare. Arnold. 1s. 9d. and 2s.
Plain Text Shakespeare. Collins. 10d.
New Readers' Shakespeare. Harrap. 1s. and 1s. 6d.
Companion Shakespeare Series. Christophers. 1s. 8d.
> *With commentaries and questionnaires after scenes, and acting notes.*

London Series of English Texts. Univ. of London Press. 1s. 9d. to 2s.
Pitt Press Series. [Ed. Verity.] Cambridge Univ. Press. 2s. 6d., 2s. 9d.

H. Literary History and Criticism

Albert. A Short History of English Literature. Harrap. 2s. 6d.
Compton Rickett. A Primer of English Literature. Nelson. 1s. 9d.
Cowling. A Preface to Shakespeare. Methuen. 5s.
Pritchard. Studies in Literature. Harrap. 2s. 6d.
> *Recommended by many correspondents.*

Elias. Great Names in English Literature. Harrap. 2 vols. 2s. each.
> *Representative extracts.*

Blakeney. Rapid Survey of English Literature. Blackie. 2s. 6d.
> *Extracts in chronological order with a good introduction.*

Rahtz. English Literature. Methuen. 3s. 6d.
> *A short comprehensive hand-book.*

Hudson. Outline History of English Literature. Bell. 4s.
> *Well-chosen representative extracts.*

Long. English Literature. Illustrated. Ginn. 7s. 6d.
> *A well-prepared summary; biographies of authors with occasional extracts.*

Pancoast. Introduction to English Literature. Bell. 7s. 6d.
> *Well-written account of the greater authors.*

Hudson. Introduction to the Study of Literature. Harrap. 6s.
> *Excellent for advanced courses.*

English Language and Literature. Chambers. Limp cloth, 1s.
> *Useful as a note-book in advanced courses.*

C. L. Thomson. A First Book of English Literature. In Seven Parts. 3s. to 4s. each. Marshall.

J. Books for Teachers

Fowler. A Dictionary of Modern English Usage. Oxford Univ. Press. 7s. 6d.
> *Already so well known that it hardly needs praise.*

Pritchard. Training in Literary Appreciation. Harrap. 2s. 6d.
Finch. How to Teach English Composition. Vols. I and II. Evans Bros. 4s. 6d. each.
Marjorie Gullan. Spoken Poetry in the Schools. Methuen. 3s. 6d.
Drury. Verse Composition for Children. Harrap. 2s. 6d.
Crump. A Guide to the Study of Shakespeare. Harrap. 2s.
Sampson. English for the English. Cambridge Univ. Press. 2s. 6d.
"Q." On the Art of Writing. Cambridge Univ. Press. 5s.

"Q." On the Art of Reading. Cambridge Univ. Press. 5s.
Lamborn. The Rudiments of Criticism. Oxford Univ. Press.
  3s. 6d.
Tomkinson. The Teaching of English. Oxford Univ. Press.
  4s. 6d.
Nicklin. The Sounds of Standard English. Oxford Univ. Press.
  2s. 6d.
Drew. Standard Speech and English Practice. Blackie. 2s. 6d.
Ratcliff. English in Upper Forms. Nelson. 2s. 6d.
S.P.E. Tracts. Nos. 11, 13–18. Oxford Univ. Press.
Warner. On the Writing of English. Blackie. 2s. 9d.
  A useful book for the master.

Macpherson. Comparative Prose. Blackie. 1s. 6d.
Macpherson. Comparative Poetry. Blackie. 1s. 6d.
  A useful companion to other collections.

Board of Education Circular, 1924. Suggestions on the Teaching
  of English.
Departmental Report on the Teaching of English in England.
Downs. English Literature. The Rudiments of its Art and
  Craft. Hodder and Stoughton. 3s. 6d.
Lamborn. Expression in Speech and Writing. Oxford Univ.
  Press. 3s. 6d.
Jagger. Modern English (Lectures to Teachers). Univ. of
  London Press. 5s.
Williams. First Steps to Parnassus. (The Craft of Poetry.) Univ.
  of London Press. 3s. 6d.
Ward. Aspects of the Modern Short Story. Univ. of London
  Press. 7s. 6d.
  Deals with some twenty short story writers.

K. Dictionaries

Annandale. A Large-type Concise English Dictionary. Blackie.
  7s. 6d.
  One of the best at the price that we know.

Collins's Dictionary of Synonyms. 1s. 6d.
Pocket Oxford Dictionary. 3s. 6d.
Cunliffe's Etymological Dictionary. Blackie. 1s. 6d.
Chambers's Etymological Dictionary. 2s.
Macmillan's Modern Dictionary. 3s. 6d.
Macmillan's Shorter Modern Dictionary. 2s.
Concise Oxford Dictionary. 7s. 6d.
Chambers's Twentieth Century Dictionary. 7s. 6d.
Collins's Etymological Dictionary. 1s. 6d.
Nelson's Highroads Dictionary. 1s. 6d.

Printed in the United States
By Bookmasters